SECRETS FROM ANCIENT GRAVES

SECRETS FROM

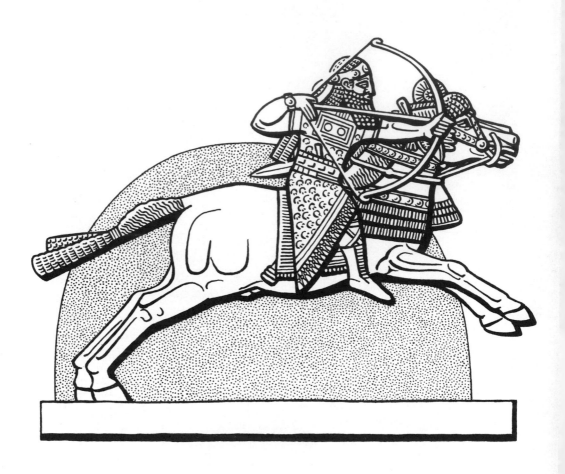

Illustrated by Eliza McFadden

ANCIENT GRAVES

DANIEL COHEN

RULERS AND HEROES OF THE PAST
WHOSE LIVES HAVE BEEN REVEALED
THROUGH ARCHAEOLOGY

Dodd, Mead & Company · New York

TO MY MOTHER

INTRODUCTION

THE INSPIRATION for this book was a statement by one of Britain's leading archaeologists, Sir Mortimer Wheeler, ". . . the archaeologist is digging up, not things, but people. Unless the bits and pieces with which he deals be alive to him . . . he had better seek out other disciplines . . ."

In the following chapters are presented the biographies of ten men and women from widely scattered times and places whose lives have been uncovered or illuminated by archaeology.

The statistics of the Great Pyramid of Egypt or of the Great Wall of China are fascinating in their own right, but far more fascinating, it seems to me, are the character and motives of the men who could order such colossal constructions. The numerous cultural levels uncovered in the excavations at Ur are of great importance to the scholar, but what the ordinary person is going to remember is how the archaeologists were able to determine that scores of Queen Shub-ad's household, dressed in their best clothes, walked calmly into her grave, and were buried with their royal mistress.

Archaeology has often been compared to detective stories. Clues are gathered from bits and pieces of evidence, and slowly a case is built up. But unlike the fictional detective who is able to wrap everything up into a solution on the last page, the archaeologist finds that large chunks of evidence are still missing. There are no neat solutions. At any moment new finds may completely alter the picture. So, in a sense, none of these biographies is really finished, nor will they ever be finished.

7

It often happens that the more we discover, the deeper and more intriguing the puzzle becomes. As long as the stories of the Mexican god Quetzalcoatl were thought to be mere folk tales, the inconsistencies and contradictions in them were unimportant. Legends are often inconsistent and contradictory. But when archaeologists discovered that there was a real, historical Quetzalcoatl, then there were many questions that had to be answered, and no answers were available.

In thinking about the ten people discussed in this book there is a great deal of scope for the exercise of judgment and imagination. But it is important not to wander too far beyond what we actually know. There are two extremes which must be guarded against: First, just because these people lived in a distant place or a very long time ago, there is no reason to view them as some other species. King Khufu and the Emperor Ch'in Shih Huang Ti were not superhuman monsters, nor were the people who labored on the Great Pyramid or the Great Wall, mindless robots. On the other hand, we must avoid the comfortable assumption that all these ancient people were just like you and me. Clearly, they were not. If Ramses II is thought of in modern terms, he becomes little more than a bragging politician, a figure of derision. But the Egyptians regarded Ramses as a god, and there is no reason to doubt that Ramses fully and honestly shared their opinion. This puts all the Pharaoh's bombast in a different light, and it is unfair to judge him by modern standards.

A little over a century ago we didn't know much about the ancient world. The histories of the Greeks and Romans had been partially recorded; the pyramids and other Egyptian monuments were there for everyone to see, although we had only a foggy notion of who built them and why. That was just about all. Archaeology began as treasure hunting. Collectors scoured the world to find ancient art objects to decorate the homes of wealthy Europeans. Then came the romantics, enthusiastic young men like Austen Henry Layard who wandered about the Middle East, "scarcely leaving untrod one spot hallowed by tradition, or unvisited one ruin consecrated by history . . .” With astonishing speed treasure hunting and romantic wandering evolved into genuine scientific exploration. In a very real way, what the archaeologists discovered changed our view of ourselves. Says archaeologist Jacquetta Hawkes, “The long vista which we now command . . . enables us to watch past effort and achievement accumulating to form the present. Archaeology has revealed the cultural evolution of man.”

Cities that had been mere names in the Old Testament were scraped from beneath the sands of the Middle East. In some cases mythical heroes of the Greeks or of the Central American Indians turned out to be real people. Whole civilizations, like the Sumerians and the Hittites, whose existence we had barely suspected, were revealed to us. The archaeologists even found out that archaeology itself was not new. The Egyptians were fanatic collectors and preservers of the past, and one Assyrian monarch had gathered a great library full of ancient documents.

A few words must be said about why these particular ten individuals were chosen. With the exception of Leif Ericsson, they are all royal personages, and Leif himself was a chieftain if not a king. I have no particular partiality to royalty, but monarchy, in one form or another, has been the system under which most people lived for the bulk of human history. Therefore, the lives of kings and queens are usually more significant than those of ordinary folk. Not always, of course; Daedalus, the legendary master builder for King Minos of Crete, may well have been more significant and interesting than his royal master. But we cannot be sure he really existed. It is the kings who build the monuments and sign the documents that archaeologists find. The lives of the ordinary people can be outlined in a general way; indeed, much of modern archaeology is aimed at bringing into focus the daily lives of the people of ancient times. But it is impossible to catch more than a fleeting glimpse of the personal life of a common man in an ancient society.

I have tried to pick people from widely varying times and places. As a result, the nature and completeness of the evidence presented varies greatly from chapter to chapter. On one hand, there are no written records about the reign of Queen Shub-ad. All we have is the archaeological reconstruction of a single climactic, terrible and revealing event. On the other hand, the Emperor Ch'in Shih Huang Ti's life is abundantly documented, but the archaeological exploration of the fantastic tales of his life is surprisingly meager. We must move gingerly from the stories to the bits of hard evidence to arrive at some sort of assessment of this formidable fellow. Most of the other chapters lie in between these two extremes. But there are no neat, complete packages. The lives of all of these people remain fruitful areas for future study or, if you prefer, they all retain an element of mystery.

A word must be said about the spelling of ancient names. All the names are transliterated; that is, the names are changed from the characters of another alphabet into the letters used in the English language. Unfortunately the transliterated spellings often do not agree. Usually, however, the spellings are quite similar. For example, the builder of the third pyramid at Giza is known as Menkure, Menkaure, Mykerinos, or Mycerirus. But the builder of the Great Pyramid, the king we call Khufu, who represented his name in hieroglyphics with pictures of the sun, two birds, and a slug, was called Cheops by the Greeks. That name is still used today, but I have tried to pick the most widely used modern spellings. Inevitably some confusion may result.

CONTENTS

CHAPTER ONE

SHUB-AD

Queen of the First Civilization

ONE OF THE COURT LADIES was slow in dressing for the great ceremony. She did not have time to put the silver ribbon around her elaborate wig, so she slipped it, still tightly coiled, into the pocket of her bright red woolen robe, and rushed off to join the gaily dressed throng that had gathered just outside the city.

The noted British archaeologist Sir Leonard Woolley reconstructed the above event when he found the coiled hair ribbon on the five thousand-year-old skeleton of a woman buried in "the great death pit at Ur." The lady was only one of sixty-eight court women who were sacrificed as part of the ghastly ritual surrounding the burial of their ruler. Sixty-seven of the women had had ribbons; traces of them were in place. They had all been dressed exactly alike, and their bodies were arranged so symmetrically that the single missing ribbon seemed odd. Upon closer examination Woolley found what looked like a lump of metal, about pocket height on the skeleton. When cleaned, this lump turned out to be the missing ribbon.

This sacrificial ritual was repeated over and over again, but the names of the royal persons whose deaths touched off the mass slaughter are, for the most part, lost forever. The only one whose

13

name we can definitely connect with a body in the royal cemetery is a woman, Queen Shub-ad. As we shall see, chance has given her a uniquely important place in history.

Woolley made his great and grim discoveries at Ur, a city famous in the Old Testament as "Ur of the Chaldees," the birthplace of Abraham. When the Old Testament was written, Ur was located in an area called Chaldea, after the tribe that ruled the land. But twenty centuries B.C., when Abraham lived there, the Chaldeans had not yet emerged into the light of history, and by Abraham's time Ur already had two thousand years of history behind it. Queen Shub-ad had lain entombed, and probably forgotten, in the cemetery outside the city for up to a thousand years before Abraham was born.

Archaeologists estimate that the city of Ur had flourished for a total of four thousand years before it was finally abandoned forever. Looking at the site of Ur today it is impossible to imagine how anyone ever lived there. Writes Woolley, "The transformation of a great city into a tangle of shapeless mounds shrouded in drift sand or littered with broken pottery and brick is not easy to understand, but it is yet more difficult to realize that the blank waste ever blossomed and bore fruit for the sustenance of a busy world." The once great city is now covered by the desert. No people are able to live there, and no vegetation breaks the monotony of barren sand. What caused this drastic change?

Ur is located in the part of the world the Greeks called Mesopotamia, the land between the rivers. It is a name modern historians still use. The rivers are the Tigris and Euphrates, which meander sluggishly across the flat Arabian plain on their way to the Persian Gulf. The fertility of Mesopotamia is entirely dependent on the river water, for the area has almost no rainfall. Ur was built in the delta of the Euphrates near the Gulf. For centuries the river carried rich silt from its upper reaches and deposited it in the delta. The build-up of silt turned the delta into a reed-filled marsh, but the

Queen Shub-ad

richness of the soil quickly attracted immigrants to the valley.

All over Mesopotamia people established themselves in little city states. A condition of eternal warfare existed between the cities, with first one then another gaining temporary supremacy. Early in the history of the land, Ur established itself as one of the most powerful cities. But warfare between the states was secondary to the efforts to wrest a living from the hostile land. The first task was to prepare the area for cultivation. At its height, Mesopotamia was crisscrossed with a network of channels for drainage of the marshes and for irrigation of the drier parts of the land. Somewhere around 300 B.C. the Euphrates burst its banks in a disastrous flood and cut a new bed for itself some eleven miles to the east. The catastrophe ruined the old water supply system and the country was too poor and disrupted at the time to construct a new system. The plain was

15

now left unwatered and at the mercy of the scorching Arabian sun. The clogged channels were turned into brackish backwaters which soon dried out, turning the land into the salt-parched desert it remains today. Ur was left stranded to decay and be forgotten.

The name "Ur of the Chaldees" was preserved in the holy books of the Hebrews, but the location of the city had been forgotten. Forgotten, too, were the remarkable Sumerians who had first brought the city to greatness.

It was not until the seventeenth century that archaeologists began to explore the history of Mesopotamia. In 1854 J. E. Taylor, a British government official serving in the Middle East, was commissioned by the British Museum to investigate some of the areas of southern Mesopotamia which might contain interesting archaeological treasures. At that point treasure hunting was still an important part of archaeology. One of the places Taylor visited was a mass of sandy mounds and debris that the Arabs called al Muqayyar, "the mound of pitch," because above the highest mound rose broken walls of red brick set in pitch mortar. Taylor dug up cylinders of baked clay covered with inscriptions which identified al Muqayyar as the site of Ur of the Old Testament.

Despite the obvious importance of the discovery, the site was ignored for another sixty years. Not until 1922, when a joint expedition of the British Museum and the University of Pennsylvania began regular excavations, was Ur's long history uncovered. Excavations continued until 1934. When the field work ended, most of the city still remained untouched. In twelve years the archaeologists had found so much material that they needed time to study it and publish their findings. The most important result of the years of work was that the existence of a hitherto unknown race—the Sumerians—was firmly established. To these mysterious people fell the honor of being the first known civilization in all human history. Our own civilization today has its roots in the land of Sumer.

The discovery of the Sumerians did not come entirely as a sur-

Sculpture of a Sumerian ruler

prise. Scholars who had deciphered the written language of later Mesopotamian peoples doubted that the complicated language could have appeared suddenly. They theorized that the wedge-shaped script had been invented by an unknown and very early people. The French archaeologist Jules Oppert called these unknown people Sumerians because the earliest known ruler of southern Mesopotamia had called himself "King of Sumer and Akkad." But when Oppert made his daring deduction, only the name was known; not a single piece of solid evidence for the existence of the Sumerians as a distinct people had been uncovered. The excavations at Ur brilliantly confirmed Oppert's educated guess.

Yet today the puzzle of the Sumerians is far from solved. These people must have come to the Euphrates delta as invaders from another land, and they must have already reached a high degree of

17

civilization before they came, for even the earliest traces of the Sumerians in Mesopotamia indicate that their culture was fully developed. But where did it develop? So far, we have been able to find no trace of them before they reached Mesopotamia. Yet some features of Sumerian culture have allowed the scholars to develop theories.

The chief feature of any Sumerian city was an enormous artificial hill called a ziggurat, on the top of which the gods were worshipped. The Biblical tower of Babel was the ziggurat of Babylon. The gods themselves were often pictured as standing on mountains. There are no mountains in Mesopotamia; it is one of the flattest places on earth. It seems reasonable, therefore, to assume that the Sumerians came from a mountainous area, perhaps the Iranian highland, or from the Asiatic mountain country farther to the east and north. But what were the conditions that inspired these people to become the first organized civilization? This is a fascinating problem that awaits future solution.

Long after the Sumerians disappeared, Mesopotamian chroniclers tried to set down the names of the rulers of their land, starting from the time of the beginning of the monarchy. Obviously many of the earliest kings on the list are mythological, for they are credited with reigns of two thousand years and more. This reflected a common Middle Eastern belief that man had passed through a golden age when people lived much longer and possessed supernatural powers. Because of this, scholars at first assumed that the entire Sumerian king list was a fable. It was Leonard Woolley who was able to link this list to archaeological record and bring Sumer into established history.

Woolley was supervising excavations at Tell al 'Ulbad, less than five miles from Ur, when one of his diggers handed him a gray soapstone covered with very ancient writing. Woolley gave the stone to C. J. Gadd, an expert in ancient languages who was standing close by. Gadd, usually a reserved man, was triumphant. The text was simple enough. "A-anni-padda, King of Ur, son of Mes-anni-padda, King of Ur, has built this for Ninkhursag, his Lady."

"But," said Woolley, "Mes-anni-padda was recorded as the first king of that First Dynasty of Ur which scholars had rejected as a mythological invention. And here was his name and that of his son on a contemporary document to prove that the supposed myth was sober history; we had rescued a whole period from oblivion and carried back the history of Ur by many hundreds of years."

There was plenty of treasure to be found at Ur, as well as the significant piece of gray stone. As Woolley's workmen dug into the royal cemetery there were moments when it seemed as if gold almost oozed out of the ground. Miraculously the tomb robbers had not stolen it all, although the cemetery had been disastrously plundered in ancient times. The robbers, however, must have been careless or frightened; they destroyed much, but enough remained to give the modern world a stunning picture of the wealth and sophistication of ancient Sumer. Still, gold was not scattered on the surface. Such discoveries came only after months of patient digging and repeated disappointments.

The royal cemetery was both a rewarding and difficult place for archaeologists to work. It had been used for hundreds of years and was honeycombed with graves. At times, as many as six grave shafts were superimposed upon one another. Graves of common people outnumbered those of royalty a hundred to one. The position of the simple contents of each had to be carefully recorded before digging could continue. Without such records it would have been impossible to establish the chronology of the cemetery. Woolley and his companions were working in the dark; there was nothing against which they could check the dates of their finds.

The first royal tomb they discovered had been thoroughly plundered. But, digging in another part of the cemetery, workmen found a layer of stone slabs. Says Woolley, "This was an astonishing thing, because there is no stone in the Euphrates delta, not so much

19

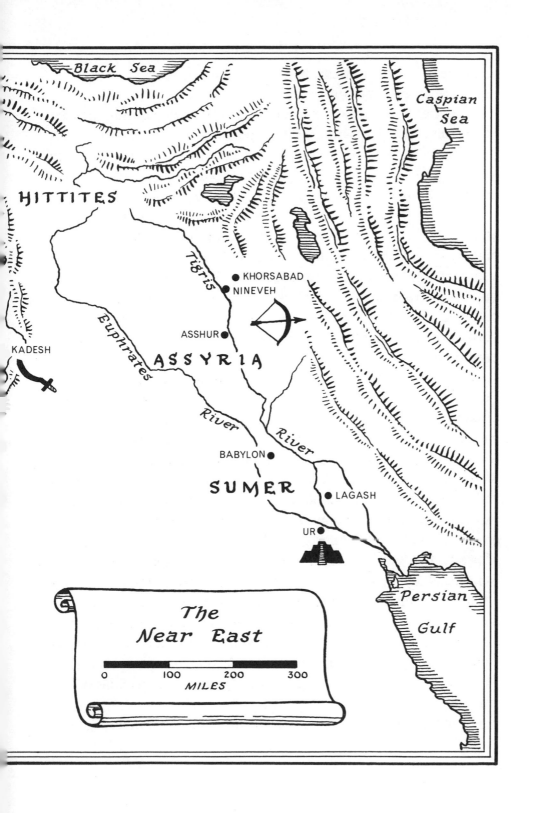

Black Sea

Caspian Sea

HITTITES

Tigris

KHORSABAD
NINEVEH

Euphrates

ASSHUR

KADESH

ASSYRIA

River

River

BABYLON

SUMER

LAGASH

UR

Persian Gulf

The Near East

0   100   200   300
MILES

as a pebble . . . To obtain blocks of limestone such as these it is necessary to go some thirty miles."

At that point work had to stop because digging during the heat of the summer is impossible in Mesopotamia. As the archaeologists thought about their discovery they became greatly excited, for they came to the conclusion that they had not found a pavement or floor, as originally believed, but rather that they had struck the roof of a tomb. Since construction with stone was an unheard-of extravagance at Ur, they felt that it must be an important tomb indeed. Autumn digging in 1927 began with high hopes. The find did turn out to be a tomb, but there was another disquieting discovery. A rubbish-filled tunnel led from near the surface to the broken roof. The robbers had been there first, and had virtually swept the tomb bare of important objects. Another disappointment! Had the entire cemetery been plundered?

Soon after this letdown the diggers found five skeletons lying side by side in a sloping trench. This was the first hint of the grisly discovery that lay beyond. It was clear that these skeletons were connected with a major burial and not in graves of their own, for aside from copper daggers at the side of each skeleton, and a few cups, there were none of the usual grave furnishings. Each of the bodies had been carefully laid out on reed matting and as the archaeologists carefully traced the remains of the matting they came upon another group of skeletons. These were ten gorgeously dressed women, whose bodies had been arranged in rows. Again the archaeologists were struck by the oddity that aside from the jewels and clothes and a few other small items, the burial contained no tomb artifacts. At the end of the row were the remains of a splendid gold and jewel-inlaid harp. The wood had decayed, but the position of all the ornamentation was intact and an accurate reconstruction was possible. The bones of the gold-crowned harpist lay across the remains of her instrument.

Proceeding farther into what the archaeologists now began to

22

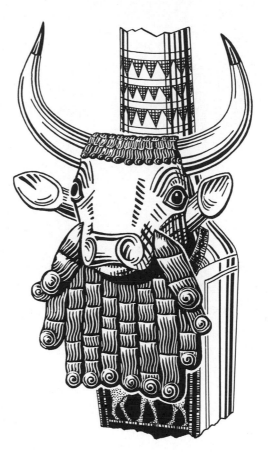

Ornamental detail of bull's head from harp

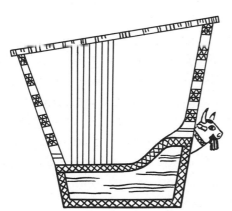

Bull-headed harp from the death pit

call the "death pit," they found more bones, not all human; another puzzle. But when they uncovered the remains of a small chariot, the meaning became clear. The animal bones belonged to a pair of asses which had pulled the chariot. The bones of the grooms lay at the heads of the animals.

The digging continued and more skeletons and heaps of precious objects were found, but nowhere was there a body set apart from the rest as obviously the person to whom all this was dedicated. As the bones and treasures of the crowded pit were cleared, the excavators struck a layer of bricks which had formed the roof to an underground stone chamber. This, it seemed, was the site of the main burial. But in ancient times the roof had been broken through and the inner chamber plundered. The archaeologists even found a wooden chest the robbers had dragged across the opening in the roof in an attempt to hide their deed. The only evidence to indicate the name of the chief person in the tomb was a cylinder seal with the inscription, A-bat-gi.

Still, it did not make sense. Why had the robbers plundered the main chamber, while leaving so much gold in the death pit? This puzzle was solved by the discovery of a second stone chamber next to the first. Atop the chamber was a cylinder with the name, Shub-ad. Woolley believed that this chamber had been built for a queen at a somewhat later period than the king A-bat-gi's tomb chamber. The exciting thing about the find was that the queen's chamber had not been robbed. All the objects that had been so carefully placed there centuries ago remained. The discovery of an unplundered royal tomb anywhere in the world ranks as a major archaeological event.

Woolley describes the scene thus: "At one end, on the remains of a wooden bier, lay the body of the queen, a gold cup near her hand; the upper part entirely hidden by a mass of beads of gold, silver, lapis lazuli, carnelian, agate, and chalcedony." There were gold pins in the form of seated gazelles and golden amulets in the form of fish.

24

On the remains of the skull was an enormous headdress, an exaggerated version of the types found earlier on the court ladies. It contained combs, bands, rings, flowers, and leaves, all of gold. Although badly crushed—for the roof of the chamber had fallen in from the weight of the earth above—Woolley's wife was able to reconstruct the headdress.

This second chamber helped the archaeologists piece together the sequence of events during the robbery of the royal cemetery. The king had been the first to die. When the queen died she was to be buried as near her husband as possible. While the workmen were preparing the second chamber they were unable to resist the lure of the rich treasure that lay just beneath their feet. They broke through the roof of the king's chamber and took out the treasure, dragging a wooden clothes chest across the hole they had made in order to hide their crime. The robbers could not touch the gold in the death pit without being detected, nor would they have been able to remove any of the queen's treasure, for it had not yet been placed in the tomb. The camouflage worked and remained undiscovered for thousands of years.

The mass slaughter that marked the funeral of Queen Shub-ad and her husband was not an isolated event. The next year an even larger death pit was found, containing the bodies of six men and sixty-eight women. The bodies of the women were arranged in regular rows, each lying on her side with legs slightly bent and hands brought up near the face. Fragments of cloth were found showing that the women wore bright red woolen robes.

Woolley concluded that there is no reason to believe that there was anything cruel or brutal about the manner in which the royal retinue died. Quite the contrary. Woolley comments on ". . . the neatness with which the bodies were laid out, the entire absence of any signs of violence or terror."

It is unlikely that they were killed and thrown into the pit, or even killed outside the grave and carried down into it with all their

Diagram of the death pit

delicate ornaments intact. It seems most probable that the victims walked calmly into the pit, took some sort of drug or poison, perhaps from the cups that were found, and lay down peacefully to give final service to their master. To die for the ruler in this way might have been considered a privilege, and a passport to a better afterlife than otherwise might have been expected. Before the pit was filled with earth some priests may have walked among the inert forms making sure that everything was in order, perhaps arranging some disordered beads, or placing the harpist's hands on the strings of her instrument.

26

Says Woolley, "It must have been a very gaily dressed crowd that assembled in the open mat-lined pit for the royal obsequies, a blaze of colour with the crimson coats, the silver, and the gold; clearly these people were not wretched slaves killed as oxen might be killed, but persons held in honour, wearing their robes of office, and coming, one hopes, voluntarily to a rite which would in their belief be but a passing from one world to another."

There is one final troublesome question. Why did the Sumerians, first men to cross the threshold of civilization, practice mass human sacrifice? There can be no final answer here. Other peoples have had such practices. The tombs of the earliest Egyptian Pharaohs indicate that the king's household joined him in death. This ritual did not last long in Egypt, and the real members of the royal household were soon replaced by small pottery figures, which were magically to assume the function of living men. In later times Scythians and Mongols and even the semi-barbaric Comans, who lived in southern Russia as late as the thirteenth century A.D., would slaughter an entire court when the king died. But of all the kingdoms of Mesopotamia, the only evidence of such burial practices had been found in Ur.

Egyptian kings were held to be living gods, and it is not so strange for a people to consider it right and proper to die for a god. But what makes the death pits at Ur so difficult to understand is that the later kings of Mesopotamia were secular rulers, although sometimes they also assumed priestly functions. Despite all their tremendous power the Mesopotamian kings were considered human. Even the greatest rulers of later times lived in abject terror of the fierce and awesome gods of Mesopotamia. The kings were above ordinary men, but far below the gods.

There is no evidence of how the people of Shub-ad's time regarded their rulers. Woolley believed that the kings and queens of the royal cemetery were gods, or at least "substitute gods" to their people. His theory is not universally accepted; in fact, some scholars doubt that Shub-ad and the others were royal personages at all. However, one interesting bit of evidence has turned up that seems to support Woolley's original thesis. A Sumerian epic poem about the great hero Gilgamesh tells of him going to his grave with his entire retinue. Gilgamesh was a semi-divine figure and the story of his adventures is filled with mythical events. But the story of Gilgamesh may also have a basis in history; he was very probably a real king and the myths surrounding his life were added later. It is significant that the epic clearly indicates the godlike status of Gilgamesh. He is believed to have died at about the same time as Meskalam-dug, one of the kings whose empty tomb was found in the royal cemetery.

Scattered hints and educated guesses are all we have to explain the death pits in the royal cemetery at Ur. Through careful work archaeologists have brought to light a magnificent and macabre fragment of human history at the crucial moment when man was first becoming civilized. To those of us living today, Shub-ad and the others at Ur seem remote, mysterious and utterly beyond our comprehension. Perhaps they are, but it is more likely that they only seem so because we know of them only at the moment of their deaths. Future discoveries may fill in the picture so that we can understand the motives of the talented Sumerians better.

CHAPTER TWO

KHUFU

Builder of the Great Pyramid

"THE SMALL PIECE of desert plateau opposite the village of Gizeh [just south of modern Cairo], though less than a mile across, may well claim to be the most remarkable piece of ground in the world. There may be seen the very beginning of architecture, the most enormous piles of buildings ever raised, the most accurate constructions known, the finest masonry and employment of the most ingenious tools . . ." So wrote W. M. Flinders Petrie, the great British archaeologist, who in the 1880's became the first man to conduct a thorough scientific exploration of the monuments at Giza, and most particularly of the Great Pyramid.

"The Great Pyramid," said Petrie, "has lent its name as a sort of by-word for paradoxes; and as moths to a candle, so are theorisers attracted to it . . . the subject was so generally familiar, and yet so little was accurately known about it."

Through the work of Petrie and others we now know much about the Great Pyramid. It is the tomb of the mighty Khufu, king of Upper and Lower Egypt. It is an artificial mountain, nearly 500 feet high and over 750 square feet at the base. It is the largest tomb ever built and the largest structure of any kind to be built until the introduction of modern machinery. For forty-five centuries Khufu's

29

tomb has remained an object of wonder and fascination.

What manner of man could wield the power to order the construction of such a monument? What kind of nation would build it for him? Khufu was king, or Pharaoh, of Egypt from about 2592 to 2569 B.C. Pharaoh is the Biblical term for the kings of Egypt; it simply means palace or great house. Khufu was the second king of the Fourth Dynasty of the Old Kingdom. Now what does all that mean?

Late in Egypt's long history a Greek historian named Manetho compiled a list of all the kings who had ever ruled that land. Manetho's list was a very long one, and for the early kings he had to rely on information that was quite vague, so the list wasn't very accurate. Today, we don't even have the original list. Historians have pieced it together from sections quoted by other writers. Manetho divided the kings of Egypt into dynasties. Each dynasty is supposed to represent the rule of a different "house" or royal family. Sometimes Manetho seems to start a new dynasty for no apparent reason; at other points he continues a dynasty when it seems clear that the throne has been usurped by a new group. But with all its shortcomings Manetho's list is the best available.

Egyptian history is further divided into the Old Kingdom, Middle Kingdom, and Empire. These are the three periods of prosperity and stability. They are separated by the First Intermediate Period, where the central authority of the king collapsed and Egypt was fragmented into a mass of hostile little states, and the Second Intermediate Period, where much of Egypt was conquered by Asiatic invaders.

Manetho's list begins with King Menes who lived around 3000 B.C. Menes' great accomplishment was to unify Egypt. Before him there were two Egypts, the south kingdom or Upper Egypt and the northern, delta kingdom or Lower Egypt. The names are confusing, because they are the exact opposite of what appears on the map. Upper Egypt is on the lower part of the map and vice versa. But the

The three pyramids at Giza

names make perfect sense in Egypt, for they are drawn from the River Nile upon which all life in Egypt depends. Upper Egypt is upstream; lower Egypt, downstream. Menes was a king of Upper Egypt, who conquered the country to the north and set up his capital at the city of Memphis on the boundary between the two states.

The next important names we come across in Egyptian history are those of King Zoser and his vizier, or chief bureaucrat, Imhotep. Zoser was the first king of the Third Dynasty and the first in the long line of pyramid builders.

The kings before Zoser were buried beneath boxlike structures called mastabas. Zoser, in fact, had a mastaba constructed for his own burial. Then Imhotep stepped in to design a grander tomb. The vizier started by building an unusually large mastaba and putting three successively smaller ones on top of it. When this was finished Imhotep was still not satisfied, so he changed the plan by enlarging the original structure and adding two more mastabas. The result was the aptly named step pyramid, located at Saqqara, fifteen miles from the center of Cairo.

After Zoser, the kings of Egypt continued to build pyramids for their tombs. But perhaps because the projects lacked a driving genius like Imhotep to guide them, most of the structures were either left unfinished or were so poorly constructed that the passage of time has reduced them to mounds of rubble.

The last king of the Third Dynasty, King Huni, built what is probably the first true pyramid. His architects started with a step pyramid, then filled in the steps. The king who followed Huni was Seneferu, Khufu's father. He was one of those lucky monarchs who has been able to retain an excellent reputation throughout all history. Long after Seneferu's death the people of Egypt told stories of his wisdom, kindness, and virtue. When an Egyptian wanted to talk about "the good old days," he talked of "the days of Seneferu."

For a final resting place Seneferu built not one pyramid, but two, a situation that caused a great deal of confusion for generations of archaeologists. Ancient documents stated quite clearly that Seneferu had two pyramids, but they did not say which two of Egypt's many unidentified pyramids they were. It took a great deal of work to identify the proper structures.

Why did Khufu's father build two tombs? In which pyramid was the king's mummy ultimately deposited? Neither of these questions can be answered satisfactorily. In fact, there is no real evidence that Seneferu was buried in either of his pyramids.

But the stage was now set for the construction of the most famous of all Egyptian monuments, perhaps the most famous monument in all history, the Great Pyramid at Giza.

It is not the beauty of the pyramid that makes it so celebrated, for it is no longer very beautiful. It is the Great Pyramid's sheer, massive, absolutely overpowering size. It contains approximately two and one-half million blocks averaging two and one-half tons each. Napoleon studied the pyramid when he was in Egypt and calculated that the stone from it could be used to build a three-foot wall around the whole of France. The base of the Great Pyramid covers an area equal to the combined base areas of the cathedrals of Florence, Milan, St. Peter's, St. Paul's, and Westminster Abbey.

The Pharaoh Khufu and his vizier, Hemon

Millions of pictures and drawings have been made of the Great Pyramid. In fact, you may have one in your pocket right now, for the back of the dollar bill contains a representation of this ancient Egyptian king's tomb.

There has never been any doubt that this tomb was built for Seneferu's son, Khufu. From ancient times until the present day, Egyptian guides have identified the pyramid as Khufu's tomb and his name has been found marked in red paint on many of the blocks.

The vizier Hemon, Khufu's cousin, was Master of Works and probably the man most responsible for the monumental task. (Another of Khufu's relatives, Prince Wepemnofret, bore the title of royal architect and may have helped in the project.) A statue of Hemon shows him to be a strong-featured, heavy-set fellow, the sort of tough, determined man needed for such a job.

The Great Pyramid immediately raises two questions in the

33

minds of most observers. How was it built, and why? The first is easier to answer.

Of all the tourists to visit the pyramids through the centuries the most influential was the Greek traveler and historian Herodotus, who came to Egypt in the middle of the fifth century B.C. His colorful but often inaccurate and even scurrilous account of the building of the pyramid is responsible for many of the modern misconceptions about Egypt. The Egyptian builders left no records of their feat, or if they did, the records have long since perished.

Herodotus did not see the pyramids being built. To him they were a part of ancient history, for the time in which he lived is almost as far removed from the time of Khufu as the present day is from the time of Herodotus.

According to stories Herodotus heard, 100,000 slaves toiled for twenty years to build Khufu's tomb. Modern research shows that the basic work crew on the pyramid construction consisted of about 4,000 permanent laborers. Housing for the 4,000 has been uncovered near the pyramid. During the season of the year when the Nile floods, many more workers were doubtless conscripted into construction gangs to float the great blocks of stone from the quarries and drag them to the building site. At these times the number of laborers may have approached 100,000. But the workmen were not slaves; slavery never played a major part in Egyptian history. They were mainly farmers who would have been idle during the flood season anyway. A chance to work and be fed at the king's expense might have been welcome. The king also undoubtedly pressed his army into service on the project, when they had nothing more urgent to attend to.

The cruelty toward the workmen has also been exaggerated. Egyptian foremen of the time carried long sticks and one of them has inscribed on his tomb the boast that he never struck a man hard enough to knock him down.

Many have found it almost impossible to accept the idea that

34

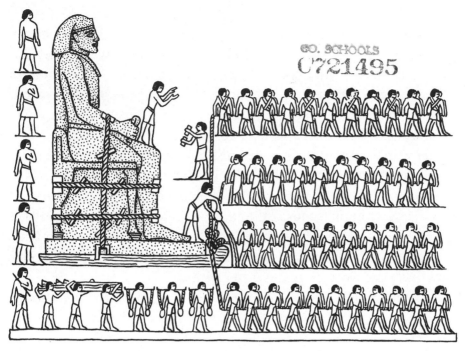

Egyptian drawing showing how heavy objects were moved

the Egyptians with their simple tools could build such a structure. Herodotus wrote of a wooden hoisting machine that the Egyptians used to get the stones of the pyramid into place. Since then, people have speculated wildly about the "mysterious pyramid lever" or about other "lost" and "mysterious" construction methods. In truth, archaeologists know a great deal about Egyptian building methods. Even if there is still some disagreement on details, none of them think that any great secrets of engineering have been lost. Aside from the Egyptians, many other ancient peoples have been able to cut and move enormous blocks of stone.

Some stones were quarried and floated for miles down the Nile on barges to the site where the king's tomb was rising slowly from the desert. Other stones were quarried nearer the pyramid and dragged in on sleds and rollers. (Wheels were rarely, if ever, used.) Eight to ten men can drag the average pyramid block weighing two and one-half tons. Each work gang seemed to have its own name. Some—the "Enduring Gang" and the "Victorious Gang"—have left their names scribbled upon the blocks they moved. As the pyramid rose in height, a ramp of mud and rubble was built up alongside it so that the blocks could be dragged to a higher tier. For a long time the idea that ramps were used in construction was mere guesswork, for they were removed when the tomb was completed. Then an early unfinished pyramid was found with the ramp still in place.

The "secret" of the pyramid builders was a generous use of ropes, levers, human muscles, and time. What seems miraculous is the patience and care these ancient builders lavished upon their task. The genius of the pyramid builders lay in their ability to organize effectively the work of great masses of men.

The Great Pyramid as we see it today is merely a ruin, although a magnificent one. Up close it looks like a series of irregular brownish steps, each about a yard high. When it was first built, however, it presented a very different appearance. Then it was sheathed in finely worked and polished white limestone blocks, so closely fitted that a knife blade could not be inserted between them. The surface was smooth and gleaming. It is doubtful if such fine workmanship could be equalled today; certainly it could not be surpassed. Sadly, all but a tiny portion of this limestone sheathing was carried away long ago and used in the construction of buildings in Cairo.

The Great Pyramid measures 756 square feet at the base. Originally it rose to a height of 480 feet, but time and vandalism have reduced its size by some 30 feet. To today's tourist the second of the three pyramids built at Giza, that of Khephren, the second king to rule after Khufu, looks, at first glance, larger than the Great Pyramid itself. That is because Khephren cheated and had his tomb built on higher ground. The smallest of the three pyramids at Giza belongs to Mykerinus, Khephren's successor.

Today the trio of Giza pyramids is surrounded by what looks like rubble. This is all that remains of the extensive complex of temples and smaller tombs that originally surrounded every pyramid.

Now why would a people lavish so much of their time, work and national treasure on the tomb of a single man? According to Herodotus, Khufu was a cruel and single-minded despot who ruined Egypt to build a monument to himself and later Egyptians hated him so much they were hardly able to speak his name. Although Khufu may have seemed a tyrant to the free-spirited Greek, the Egyptians hardly considered him one. Like his father, he was revered for centuries after his death. Nor is there any evidence that Khufu—or any other Egyptian king, for that matter—was particularly cruel. Life was harsh by modern standards, but compared to other ancient societies the Egyptians, Khufu included, were far and away the most humane of people.

There is also no solid support for the idea that the expense of building Khufu's tomb, although it must have been enormous, left Egypt bankrupt and exhausted. Two of his successors were able to build pyramids rivaling the Great Pyramid in size and magnificence.

It is important to realize that the King of Egypt was not an ordinary ruler. He was considered a god in his own right, and to the common workman the backbreaking toil of dragging huge blocks for the pyramid was a religious obligation. They believed the king-god protected the land and assured its prosperity. When strong kings like Khufu sat upon the throne, the valley of the Nile was tranquil and happy. When the kingship was weak, there was no central authority to organize the essential irrigation projects and the crops failed. Commerce up and down the river was interrupted; there was civil strife and occasionally foreign invasion. The ordinary Egyptian farmer or craftsman did not resent his lack of freedom, for the concept of individual liberty was unknown in ancient Egypt. The divinity of the king of Egypt was already established at the beginning of Egyptian history and it endured for thousands of years—longer, in fact, than any other form of government in the history of man.

The importance of preservation of the body as a part of Egyptian religion was also established early. This is probably because the dry and clean soil and air of Egypt made preservation extremely easy. The earliest Egyptians buried their ancestors in shallow graves. and they must have noticed that if the graves were opened years later the bodies retained a remarkably lifelike appearance. As the religion developed, the practice of burial became encrusted with an elaborate ritual of preparing the mummy, as the preserved linen-wrapped body is called. But the Egyptians possessed no magical or secret methods of preservation. In some cases, where mummies were covered with various preserving solutions, they actually were destroyed, while the untreated bodies endured.

It was customary for an Egyptian to be buried with many of his possessions, so he could continue to enjoy them in the afterlife. In the case of Khufu, he must have been interred with a treasure of unbelievable magnificence.

In a fundamental sense the Great Pyramid was a great failure. Its purpose was to protect Khufu's body for eternity. Yet long ago the king's mummy was reduced to the dust of the land where he had once ruled as a god. All the gold and other treasure that was buried with him was stolen and eventually melted down or altered in some other way until today nothing remains. This is not unusual, because archaeologists have estimated that 99 per cent of all ancient tombs have been plundered.

The Great Pyramid with all its riches must have been an irresistible prize for tomb robbers. Khufu's engineers cunningly sealed the interior passages with great granite blocks, and carefully disguised the entrance to the tomb. In fact, they built three chambers within the pyramid. This may have been the result of a change of plan, or two of the chambers may have been decoys to confuse the robbers. But the robbers were patient and resourceful. The Great Pyramid was probably plundered for the first time in the period of anarchy that followed the collapse of the Old Kingdom. Then there would have been no strong government to guard the resting place of

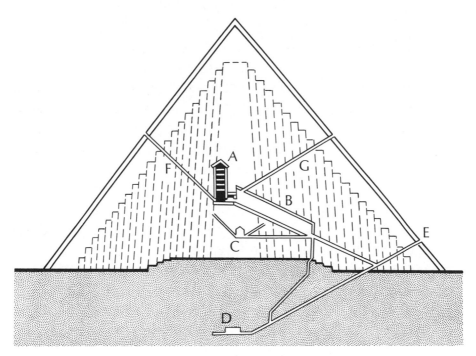

Diagram of the Great Pyramid showing: A—King's burial chamber; B—Gal-lery; C and D—Incomplete or false burial chambers; E—Entrance; F and G—Air shafts

Close-up of the king's burial chamber

the god. Perhaps the robbers enlisted the aid of corrupt priests or attendants who knew the hidden entrances. Later, when pious and strong monarchs again ruled, other mummies were placed in the empty pyramid and it was resealed. We can only guess at the number of robberies and reburials that took place in the Great Pyramid.

When the Muslims came to power in Egypt they cared nothing for the ancient traditions. To them, Khufu and all the other kings of the past lived in the "days of ignorance." In the ninth century the Caliph al-Ma mun determined to get inside the Great Pyramid. Unable to find the entrance, he simply had his workmen bore a hole through the limestone until they struck one of the interior passages. Then he destroyed what he thought was Khufu's mummy and plundered what he thought was Khufu's treasure. Both mummy and treasure dated from a much later time and must have been but a pale reflection of the opulence of the original burial. After Ma mun, the Great Pyramid remained open and empty.

Today the Great Pyramid has been measured and studied in the minutest detail. In addition it has been stared at and crawled over by literally millions of tourists. It seems impossible that anything about it could have remained undiscovered. But the sands of Giza still conceal some surprises.

In 1954, workmen building a new road were removing a mound of debris and sand at the south side of the pyramid when they uncovered the outlines of a long, sealed pit. When the pit was opened, it was found to contain a large cedar wood boat in a marvelous state of preservation. The boat measured 143 feet in length and is the oldest large boat ever found. Archaeologists speculate that it had actually been used in Khufu's funeral procession. They are hopeful of finding other boats at the site.

A still more spectacular find escaped the resourceful robbers and the observant scholars until this century. In 1925 a photographer for the Giza expedition of Harvard University set his tripod on what seemed to be solid rock. As he moved the tripod one of the legs knocked loose a chip of plaster. The area was not solid rock but a plaster covering, shaped and colored to match the rock. Beneath the plaster were large cut stones covering a shaft. The archaeologists were elated, for it was obvious that the blocks had not been disturbed since the shaft was first sealed.

To the untrained eye the contents of the chamber at the bottom of the shaft were in hopeless confusion. The furniture had been made of wood covered with sheets of gold and inlaid with ebony. During the centuries the wood had decayed and the unperishable gold and ebony collapsed on the floor. Wooden shelves that had once held vases rotted away and the vases fell and were smashed. A tomb robber would have picked out the gold and other precious materials from the debris in a few hours, and that would have been the end of it. But the archaeologists took months clearing the chamber. The placement of every scrap was carefully recorded before it was delicately and lovingly removed. Later they were able to reconstruct completely the funerary equipment, considered by many to be the finest examples of Egyptian workmanship in existence. It is now on display in the Cairo museum. Inscriptions quickly established that the objects in the chamber belonged to Queen Hetepheres, Khufu's mother.

Although no robbers had ever forced the passage, something was terribly wrong. There were too many objects for such a small chamber. It seemed as though the precious things had literally been thrown in. Everywhere there were signs of haste and sloppiness completely uncharacteristic of Egyptian royal burials.

It was not until 1928 that the sealed sarcophagus, the principal object in the tomb, was opened. The honor fell to George Reisner, head of the Harvard Expedition. Before a small group of distinguished visitors gathered in the underground room, he ordered the heavy stone lid raised and peered inside. Turning to his guests, he said, "Gentlemen, I regret Queen Hetepheres is not receiving." The sarcophagus was empty.

What had happened? Reisner had a guess. The tomb represented a reburial. Originally the queen's body had been buried somewhere else, but the original tomb had been plundered during the reign of her son and Khufu ordered the reburial. Reisner offered the theory that the king himself had never been told that his mother's body had been destroyed by the robbers, because those responsible for guarding the tomb feared the royal anger. Or perhaps Khufu felt that reburying part of the funerary equipment was better than nothing. There are other cases where an empty sarcophagus had been buried. Whatever the reason, a secret tomb was dug, and camouflaged so effectively that it remained hidden for over four thousand years. It is ironic that this small, poorly constructed tomb should have served its purpose so well, while the Great Pyramid itself remained unviolated for less than a few hundred years.

The Great Pyramid was a failure in a second fundamental way. Khufu doubtless hoped that this would assure his worship throughout the ages. Instead, it has given him, quite unjustly, the reputation of a monster. Worse still, it has helped to create the fiction that Egypt was an alien, morbid, and cheerless society. This misunderstanding has clouded our appreciation of a very talented and very human people.

CHAPTER THREE

RAMSES II

The Pharaoh Who Could Never Lose

LET US START the story of Ramses II at the end, with the dramatic and unexpected discovery of this famous king's mummy. In 1881 Mohammed Ahmed Abed-er-Rassoul, a member of a family of highly successful and wealthy tomb robbers had a falling out with his brothers. He decided to talk to Egyptian authorities, who for years had been trying to put an end to the clan's plunder of ancient treasures. That they had been unable to do so was not surprising. The Abed-er-Rassoul family had been in the tomb-robbing business since the thirteenth century. For his defection from family tradition Mohammed Ahmed Abed-er-Rassoul was given a reward of 500 pounds sterling and a job with the Egyptian government Department of Excavations and Antiquities, where it was felt his unusual skills would be of great value.

To prove his good faith the ex-tomb robber led the authorities to his family's chief discovery, a well-concealed tomb at the base of a cliff at Deir el-Bahri. The robbers had discovered their prize six years before and had been slowly selling its contents on the thriving black market in antiquities.

Emil Brugsch, a young European archaeologist working for the Egyptian government, was the first of the official party to lower himself into the narrow and sinister looking hole in the ground. After crawling through an underground passage Brugsch found himself in a large, irregular, oblong chamber crammed with a confusion of mummies, coffins, statuettes, jars, and other funerary equipment. By the flickering light of his candle he read the names on the coffins and mummies. He could hardly believe his eyes.

Later Brugsch's superior, Gaston Maspero, Director General of Excavations and Antiquities of Egypt, described what his young assistant had seen: "The report which had first seemed exaggerated hardly expressed the truth; where I had expected to find one or two minor kings, the Arabs had dug up a vault full of Pharaohs. And what Pharaohs! Probably the most famous in the history of Egypt: Thutmoses III and Seti I, Amose the Liberator and Ramesses II the Conqueror. M. Emile Brugsch thought that he must be dreaming, coming upon such an assemblage so suddenly. Like him, I still ask myself if it is true and if I am dreaming when I see and touch the bodies of all these people when we never thought to know more than their names."

What Brugsch had been shown by the robber was not an ordinary tomb, but a carefully concealed hiding place built by priests of what must have been an ancient Egyptian cult of the dead. Ramses II had certainly never intended his mummy for a common grave. He had built a fine tomb for himself in the Valley of the Kings, traditional burial place for royalty of his time. But when the tomb was threatened, or actually plundered by Abed-er-Rassoul's ancient predecessors, priests—whose job it was to see to the continued protection and worship of the dead kings—moved the mummy. These priests left a record of the wanderings of Ramses' mummy on its linen wrapping. First it was secretly moved to the tomb of his father, Seti I, then both were taken to the tomb of Queen Isimkheb. Later they were conveyed to the tomb of Amenophis I, and finally transferred to the collective tomb at Deir el-Behri, already crowded with many other royal mummies. Three thousand years later Brugsch found forty of them in the chamber.

In his description of the find of the horde of royal mummies Maspero called Ramses II, "the Conqueror." The epithet does not really fit. He is more commonly known as Ramses the Great, but this too is inaccurate. Ramses the Incredible has been suggested as a better title. A few statistics preserved in Egyptian records will show why.

Ramses was born in 1318 B.C. and came to the throne in 1298. He died in 1232 B.C. at the age of eighty-six, a really remarkable example of longevity in the ancient world. He had reigned a total of sixty-seven years, very nearly a record for any monarch of any country in any age. (The record is held by another Pharaoh, Pepy II, last ruler of the Old Kingdom, who ruled for over ninety years.)

Egyptian kings customarily had large harems. The names of seven of Ramses' wives, seventy-nine of his sons, and thirty-one of his daughters have been preserved, and this probably represents only a fraction of the total.

Ramses II was the third Pharaoh of the Nineteenth Dynasty. The Eighteenth Dynasty had ended when Haremhab, a general, usurped the throne and spent his reign trying to end the confusion that had resulted from the religious revolution of the Pharaoh Ikhnaton. Haremhab was childless at the time of his death and he chose an old comrade-in-arms, another general called Ramses, as his successor. This first Ramses was well advanced in years when he came to the throne and survived for only a year or two. He was succeeded by his son, Seti I.

When the mummies from the royal horde were unwrapped it was Seti who provided the archaeologists with their greatest shock. Obviously he had been a handsome and regal figure when alive, and his mummy was so well preserved that he looked more like a man who had just fallen asleep than a three thousand-year-old corpse. The Egyptologist, Kurt Lange, commented, "We must aver we find many persons still living who look more decayed."

45

The mummy of Seti I

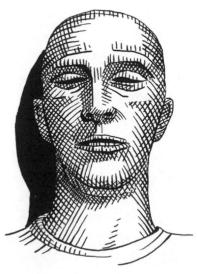

Close-up of head of mummy

Seti I was an able and vigorous ruler who set out to reconquer Egypt's lost empire. In this endeavor he had only limited success, but he passed his ambition along to his son, Ramses. In the fourth year of his reign the new Pharaoh began his military operations by conducting an inconclusive campaign in Palestine. This merely whetted his appetite for war, and the following year he planned a more ambitious enterprise. His first goal was the city of Kadesh in what is now Lebanon. Kadesh was a strongly fortified city, but Thutmosis III, most successful of all Egyptian conquerors, had taken it twice. By Ramses' time Kadesh had once again shaken off Egyptian control, and had fallen under the protection of another powerful empire—the Hittites.

Ramses marched out of Egypt at the head of a large, well-trained, well-supplied army. In a month he stood on a hill overlooking Kadesh. Somewhere nearby was the main body of the Hittite army under the command of King Muwatallis.

The battle of Kadesh is the first battle in all history that is known in detail. Ramses made certain that his exploits that day would never be forgotten; he had a long epic poem describing the battle inscribed on the walls of at least three different temples.

The poem distorts the events of the battle in order to make Ramses appear a hero, and scholars have had to do quite a bit of interpretation in order to discover what really did happen. But from the poem and other scattered hints we today have gained a reasonably clear idea of the course of the fighting at Kadesh.

As Ramses was trying to determine the whereabouts of the Hittite force, two men who said they were Hittite deserters were brought before him. They told Ramses that Muwatallis had been so terror-stricken at the approach of the Great Pharaoh that he had retreated northward in panic, leaving Kadesh unprotected. Ramses apparently had such a high opinion of himself that he believed the story without question. He split his army into four sections and personally took charge of the forward group which was marching some

47

six miles ahead of the main body of the army. The move was bold
and foolish, for Ramses did not even bother to send out an advance
scouting party. If the Hittite army were anywhere nearby, the
Pharaoh would be in great personal danger. And, as Ramses could
easily have discovered, the Hittite army was very close indeed.

The two "deserters" had been in reality Hittite spies and
Ramses was walking right into a trap that Muwatallis had cunningly
set for him. Muwatallis sent his chariot corps smashing into the rear
of the second of the four Egyptian divisions, cutting it off from the
third and fourth. In the surprise attack the entire Egyptian division
was virtually annihilated, and the Hittite army now stood between
the Pharaoh and the bulk of his army. The first Ramses knew of his
extremely perilous position was when the panic-stricken remnants
of the second division came fleeing past him.

Just exactly how Ramses managed to save his skin from what
surely would have been a catastrophic defeat is not entirely clear.
The Egyptian epic says that by superhuman efforts Ramses managed to rout the entire Hittite army singlehandedly.

"His Majesty was all alone with his bodyguards. The wretched
prince of Hatti [the Egyptian title for King of the Hittites], however, stood in the center of his own army, and for fear of His Majesty
he did not come forth in the fighting." Here, the clever Muwatallis is
blamed for not allowing himself to be trapped and isolated as
Ramses was.

"Now when the king looked behind him, he saw that he was
blocked off by 2500 chariots. All the various warriors of the
wretched king of Hatti encircled him . . ." Ramses laments. "No
prince is beside me and no chariot driver, no officer of the infantry
and none of the charioteers. My foot soldiers and my charioteers
have abandoned me to the enemy, and none of them held fast to fight
against him." Characteristically, Ramses blames everyone else for
his plight.

The Egyptian poem continues; the king invokes his god Amon,

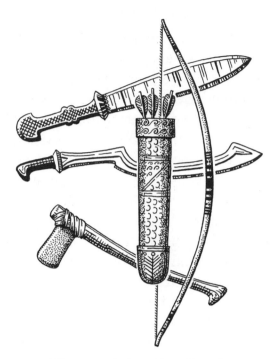

Weapons of the ancient Egyptians

and finds new strength. He cries, "I have found my heart again; my heart bursts with joy; whatever I will, is done . . . I let fly my arrows to the right and fight to the left. . . . Behold, 2500 chariots surrounded me, and now they lie hacked to pieces before my steeds. Not one of the foe could lift his hand to fight. Their hearts in their bodies grew faint for fear, and their arms sag with weakness. They cannot shoot their arrows and have not the heart to take up their spears. I make them fall into the water like crocodiles. They crash into one another and I go among them killing at will."

The accounts also briefly mention the arrival of a small detachment of Egyptian troops, known only as "boys from the land of Amurru." They may have been a regiment of auxiliary troops sent up from the coast to join the main army. It seems this detachment arrived at a critical moment. By that time the Hittite troops had probably broken rank and were busily plundering the equipment left behind by the fleeing Egyptians. Under such conditions they would have been extremely vulnerable to attack from the rear.

Ramses may indeed have fought ferociously and inspired the remainder of his retinue. Between the Pharaoh's desperate attacks and the "boys from the land of Amurru" the Hittites were unable to capture the Pharaoh by the time the last two divisions of the Egyptian army arrived at the scene of the battle. Night had already fallen and the Hittites retreated within the walls of Kadesh, leaving Ramses in possession of the battlefield and his life, but little else.

The Pharaoh gathered his scattered army and immediately retreated. Of course, the court poet never uses that word, for the mere hint that Ramses could have been anything less than totally successful was unthinkable. In the poem Ramses boasts that he had "broken the back of the Hatti forever."

While Ramses was marching rapidly homeward the Egyptian account says that "the wretchedly fallen prince of Hatti sent a message honoring the great name of His Majesty . . . 'The land of Egypt and the land of Hatti, yes, they are your servants and all lie at your feet.'" Magnanimously, however, Ramses holds out his hand in friendship and Egyptians and Hittites agree on a peace treaty.

In truth, it seems Ramses was extremely lucky to get off so easily. The land of Hatti certainly did not lie at his feet. He did not even reach the heart of the Hittite domain; rather, he began his retreat a good 375 miles away from the Hittite capital and had failed in his first objective of capturing Kadesh. Still, Ramses managed to turn the battle of Kadesh into a great propaganda victory, for home consumption. Understandably the Hittites did not see it that way at all. When Hittite references to the battle were found at their capital at Boghazköy they told of an Egyptian defeat, with Ramses losing much of the area reconquered by his father.

There is some evidence that the people of the time considered the battle of Kadesh an Egyptian defeat. Records show that Bentesina, ruler of the land of Amurru, who had become an Egyptian ally, switched to the Hittite side after the battle. It is doubtful that a Middle Eastern ruler of that day would leave the victors to join the vanquished.

Despite the treaty of peace after the battle of Kadesh, Ramses' annals tell of further victories over the Hittites. But, by the twenty-first year of Ramses' reign both countries had become weary of the inconclusive and exhausting border warfare and signed a formal treaty of peace. It is the first international treaty of which we have a full record. By wondrous coincidence, both Egyptian and Hittite versions of the treaty have survived. The Egyptian copy is carved on the walls of Ramses' mortuary temple at Karnak. The Hittite copy was found on two clay tablets dug up at Boghazköy.

The two versions differ in minor respects. Each side made the treaty sound like a great victory for them. Ramses' version, for example, is preceded by an elaborate prologue which explains how the Hittite king came pleading for peace with Ramses, "that bull among princes, who establishes the borders of his land wheresoever he will." Leaving aside the extravagant flattery— a feature of all Oriental state documents and particularly typical of any document from the court of Ramses II—the treaty has a strikingly modern ring. Both parties agreed to stop attacking one another's land, and to establish perpetual peace. They also agreed to aid one another in case of external invasion or internal revolution. The clause dealing with the status of political refugees is even more modern in tone. The Egyptian version reads:

"If a man—or even two or three—should flee from the Land of Egypt and come to the Great Prince of Hatti, let the Great Prince of Hatti take him captive and have him sent back to Ramses, the Great Lord of Egypt. But if any man is sent back to Ramses II, the Great Lord of Egypt, let him not be charged with a crime, nor shall his house or his wives and his children be harmed, nor shall he be killed or injured in any way, neither his eyes nor his ears nor his tongue nor his feet, nor shall he be charged with any crime."

51

Interior of Egyptian temple

Identical conditions applied to fugitives from Hittite lands who escaped to Egypt. What is impressive about this clause is its humanitarianism. It shows that mercy was considered a virtue by both lands. The treaty between Ramses and the Hittites provides for far more civilized treatment of prisoners than was accorded them in eighteenth century England or, for that matter, in many supposedly civilized countries today.

From all available evidence, the peace treaty was carefully observed by both parties for seventy years, giving the turbulent Middle East one of the longest tranquil periods in history.

Ten years after the pact was concluded, the friendship of the two great empires was sealed by a royal marriage, between Ramses and a daughter of the Hittite king. Ramses had outlived his early enemy, Muwatallis, and it was king Hattusilis III who sent the Pharaoh one of his daughters. Ramses inscribed his version of the marriage on a monument near his great temple of Abu Simbel. Although the Hittites had been his firm allies for almost a decade, he cannot refrain from boasting that "after the victory of Ramses II over the Land of Hatti, the latter is living in wretchedness and fear. The Great Prince sends his daughter to Ramses." According to the Egyptian scribe, the Hittites came "with fearful steps, bearing all their possessions as a tribute to the fame of His Majesty. His [the Hittite King's] eldest daughter comes before, in order to satisfy the heart of the Lord of the Two Lands."

This description of the Hittite princess as little more than an article of tribute from her defeated father to the conqueror Ramses is a gross distortion. The Hittite princess came in triumph at the head of a great armed retinue. According to the inscription Ramses was overjoyed when he heard of the approach of the Hittites and sent his army and nobles to greet them. It was an extraordinary event, "whose like was not known before in Egypt." The troops of the two countries greeted one another like old friends. "They ate and drank together; they were as harmonious as brethren between whom there are no grudges."

The tale assumes a romantic note when the meeting of Ramses and the Hittite princess is described. "She was beautiful in the eyes of his Majesty, and he loved her more than anything." All this, in the words of the Egyptian chronicler, was "A magnificent marvel . . . like nothing that is set forth in the writings of our forefathers."

The Hittite princess did not simply disappear into Ramses' vast harem. She was raised to the position of Great Chief Wife of the Pharaoh, a high position for a foreigner. She took the Egyptian name of Maatnefrure, meaning Truth is the Beauty of Re (one of Egypt's chief gods).

Ramses saw the advantages of a lasting peace with his dangerous neighbor. The Egyptian account of the marriage says, "Henceforth, when a man or a woman in the course of their affairs traveled through Syria and came to the Land of Hatti, there was no fear in their hearts because the might of His Majesty was so great." Where once Ramses had assumed all the credit for military victory, he now claimed all credit for the fruits of peace.

His marriage to the Hittite princess is the last major event in Ramses' reign for which we have any record. It appears he spent the rest of his days ruling over a stable and prosperous nation and constructing monuments to his own greater glory. To the Egyptians who lived during the time of Ramses II it must have seemed like the dawn of a new golden age. In retrospect, however, we can see that the age was bathed in the glow of the sunset of Egyptian civilization. But, as befits this great nation, the twilight was long and often magnificent.

With at least seventy-nine sons there was no problem of finding a male heir to the throne, but by the time Ramses II finally died he had already outlived twelve potential heirs. He was succeeded by his thirteenth son, Merneptah, already a middle-aged man. Egypt itself had changed little during Ramses' long reign, but stability was deceptive, for the world around had changed drastically. The Hittite nation, which had driven back the Egyptians from the field of Kadesh, was falling to pieces. Documents show that Merneptah had to send food to the beleaguered Hittite king to help him when famine ravaged his once wealthy empire. Egypt itself was attacked by a federation of nomadic nations from the north known collectively as The Peoples of the Sea. Merneptah managed to drive them back, but he could not truly defeat them, and they returned time and again to harass later kings.

Merneptah's reign ended in a period of anarchy, and a profusion of kings and even a queen sat briefly on the throne of Egypt. A new dynasty of unknown antecedents seized the throne and managed to reestablish order. The kings of this dynasty—there were nine of them—all called themselves Ramses, although any direct relationship to the "great" Ramses is doubtful.

Ramses II has often been identified as the wicked Pharaoh of the Hebrew Exodus from Egypt. There are two reasons for this: First, Ramses is far and away the best known of all the Pharaohs and therefore the most likely to be blamed for everything; second, the Bible mentions a city named Ramses, although many scholars believe this reference was inserted at a later date. Another prime candidate for this unpopular position is Ramses' son, Merneptah. One of his monuments contains the only undisputed reference to Israel that has ever been found in Egyptian records. On the back of a monument at Karnak, constructed by an earlier king, Merneptah had inscribed a commemoration of one of his own victories. In the list of the peoples the Pharaoh claimed to have crushed we find these words: "Israel is desolated and has no seed." Actually, the monument, which is known as the Israel Stela, proves that Merneptah could not possibly have been the Pharaoh at the time of the Exodus, for it indicates that the children of Israel had already left Egypt. Today, most Biblical archaeologists place the events of the Exodus at an earlier era.

The first modern Egyptologists were awed by Ramses II. The brilliant young French linguist, Jean Francois Champollion, deciphered Egyptian hieroglyphs in 1821, and eager scholars immediately set to work reading the "pictures" which had tantalized them for so long. When the poem describing the battle of Kadesh was deciphered, many scholars hailed the author as an Egyptian Homer and this outrageous piece of propaganda was favorably compared to the *Iliad*. But as the laborious task of excavation and decipherment continued to fill in the picture of Egyptian history, Ramses' reputation began to decline, until today he is regarded as more of a braggart than a great ruler. The attitude expressed by the American Egyptologist, Dr. Barbara Mertz, is typical: "I used to wonder,

55

when I listened to the tales of my acquaintances who had been fortunate enough to travel in Egypt, at the animosity they displayed to Ramses II . . . Now that I have visited Egypt myself, I can understand the reaction; I, too, snarl. One gets so tired of Ramses; his face, his figure, and/or his name are plastered over half the wall surfaces still standing in Egypt, at least it seems that way. He was probably the most monumental egoist of all time."

Yet even with this downgrading of Ramses and his works, the reputation of the Pharaoh manages to exert a powerful influence even today. When one of Ramses II's most colossal monuments, the temple of Abu Simbel, was threatened in recent years with inundation by the construction of the new high dam at Aswan, people throughout the world were shocked. Facing the loss of what had come to be considered one of mankind's greatest historical treasures, an unprecedented international salvage operation was launched under the direction of UNESCO and the United Arab Republic. Money and salvage ideas came from many sources. A large number of plans were considered for saving the temple. Finally the government of the UAR decided in favor of a plan to cut the temple into blocks, an idea conceived by a Swedish engineering firm. The blocks, weighing about 30 tons each, were to be reassembled in the neighborhood of the original site, but on higher ground to escape the waters.

Abu Simbel was not a free-standing temple. It had been cut from the solid rock; thus, the temples had to be excavated out of the cliffs into which they had been built. This meant removing some 300,000 tons of rock. No explosives could be used, for the rock of Abu Simbel was very fragile and the walls and statuary were already badly cracked. The climate of the area is extremely severe, and created great difficulty for the scores of European technicians who helped supervise the project. Accomplishing this enormously difficult task, while racing the rising waters being backed up by the dam, was a feat which rivalled the original construction of Abu Simbel.

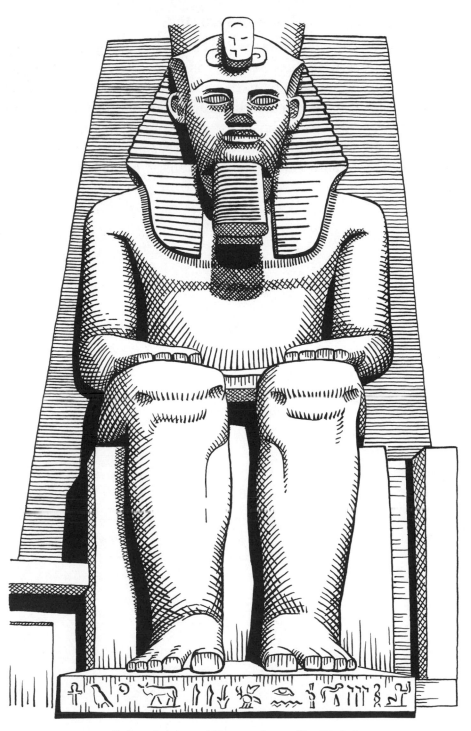

Colossal statue of Ramses from Abu Simbel

By 1967 the delicate task of excavating, cutting, and moving the temple had been successfully completed. Reconstruction on higher ground was scheduled to be finished before 1970. Ultimately the project will have cost nearly $40 million, a truly magnificent sum when one considers that most archaeological expeditions are conducted on a shoestring budget. The rescue of Abu Simbel is just the sort of grandiose enterprise that Ramses himself would have undertaken.

CHAPTER FOUR

HATTUSILIS III

The Apologetic Usurper

KING MUWATALLIS' BROTHER Hattusilis was a man to be reckoned with in the land of the Hittites. So great was his power that the king feared his brother would lead a revolt. Yet Hattusilis was such a superb general and administrator that the king did not dare remove him. When Muwatallis died his son Urhi-Teshub inherited a power-ful rival as well as the throne. Arrogant and foolish, Urhi-Teshub was a very different sort of man from his father, and soon lost the respect of his people. Hattusilis watched the young king sourly, re-maining silent until Urhi-Teshub tried to reduce the territory under his uncle's control. Then Hattusilis could stand it no longer. Quickly, meeting almost no opposition, he overwhelmed the rightful heir and made himself king, taking the title of Hattusilis III.

Up to this point there is nothing unusual about the story. Royal coups are common enough. Hattusilis, however, did two peculiar things. First, he did not have Urhi-Teshub killed, but had him sent into comfortable, although distinct, exile. Second, he sat down and wrote a long document to justify his actions. Usurpers are not usu-ally so fussy. When they bother to justify themselves at all, they either claim that they were the rightful rulers all the while or say that they acted upon the direct orders of the gods. Hattusilis would have none of such easy excuses, and the Hittite people probably would not have accepted them, for their political sophistication was truly remarkable.

The Hittites had built a great empire in the part of the world known as Asia Minor. For a time it ranked with Egypt and Babylon as the leading empire of the civilized world. Then the Hittites got lost in the shuffle of history, and only during the last eighty years have we begun to realize that they were anything more than a petty tribe.

The Old Testament contains numerous references to the Hittites, but to the scholars of the last century there seemed nothing in the Bible to indicate that the Hittites were any more important than the scores of other tribes that the Hebrews encountered. In retrospect we can see that many of the passages do indeed hint at the true scope of Hittite power, but at the time these were not interpreted correctly. Also misinterpreted were numerous and extensive Egyptian refer-

Hittite pedestal

ences to Hittites, and even the pictures of Hittites in Egyptian temple paintings. As far as the best historians of the nineteenth century were concerned, the Hittite empire had never existed.

A little over a hundred years ago European travelers began to penetrate parts of Turkey and Syria which had long been closed to them. From widely scattered places they brought back stories of strange monuments and inscriptions, or even of entire ruined cities of ancient and obscure origin. Scholars puzzled over these tales, but could make nothing of them.

Then in 1879 a thirty-year-old Orientalist, Archibald Henry Sayce, was traveling in Turkey and meditating upon the monuments and inscriptions he had seen and read about. "Suddenly the truth flashed upon me," Sayce wrote. "In all alike we had the same characteristic features, the same head-dresses and shoes, the same tunics, the same clumsy massiveness of design and characteristic attitude." When he returned to London he told his colleagues that all these far-flung remains were Hittite, and that the unimportant tribe had in reality been masters of an empire.

Scholars, even young ones like Sayce, are not supposed to make wild statements, and to most of the experts Sayce's Hittite theory sounded incredible. They could not believe it. But the young Englishman's inspiration opened the floodgates of discovery. Confirming evidence began to pour in from everywhere, and within eighty years the Hittite language was deciphered and the outlines of Hittite history emerged.

This, however, is not meant to imply that great gaps in our knowledge of Hittite history do not still exist. The biggest question is who were the Hittites and where did they come from? We believe they first came to the mountains of Asia Minor as conquerors around 2000 B.C. They were probably a small military elite who gained supremacy over the native population. What these conquerors called themselves we do not know, but it was not Hittites. This name stems from early mistranslation of some documents, but no one has been able to offer a better name, so Hittites has stuck. Earliest records show them ruling a number of city states, including one near the modern village of Boghazköy, which in later days was to become the capital of their empire.

What makes the problem of Hittite origins particularly intriguing is that they spoke what is called an Indo-European language; in fact, their language comes from the branch of Indo-European language family related to Greek, Latin, Celtic, and Germanic. At least eight distinct languages were commonly used during the period of the Hittite empire, but the basic tongue of the rulers was of Indo-European origin. The Hittites are the first important Indo-European speaking group known to history.

The oddly introspective character of the Hittites showed itself first in the person of King Hattusilis I (1650-1520 B.C.). This first Hattusilis was a successful ruler, but his family life, it seems, left much to be desired. A document attributed to the king himself tells of his sorrow during an illness.

Hattusilis' chosen successor was a foster son he called young Labarnas. But the king laments, "How the boy has behaved during my illness. It is indescribable! He shed no tears, he showed no pity. Cold he is and heartless. . . . To the words of the king he has never hearkened. But to the words of his mother, the serpent. . . . Brothers and sisters brought evil counsels to him again and again." So the king determined to disinherit the boy, but makes a point that, despite his dislike of young Labarnas, he has never done him any bodily harm.

As a political document the king's mournful testament is remarkable. It is hard to imagine an exalted Egyptian or Babylonian monarch speaking, or even thinking, in such terms.

For over a century Hittite power grew under a line of kings (including a second Hattusilis) until in 1375 B.C. the Hittites found their Alexander and the Hittite empire truly began. Suppiluliumas was not only a great war leader, but he was an exceptionally astute

Reconstruction of Hittite war chariot

politician. Hittite armies poured from their mountain strongholds, grinding tribes and nations under the wheels of their magnificent war chariots. But rather than enslaving the peoples he conquered Suppiluliumas held them to his empire by means of clever, but binding alliances.

Suppiluliumas' eldest son died of the plague after reigning only a year. He was followed by another son, Mursilis II, who proved a true offspring of his father and secured most of the latter's conquests. But what a strange warrior he was. Sickly and gloomy, he exposed the dark side of his nature in a unique work called "Prayers in Time of Plague" which ends with the line "From my heart drive out the pain, O Lord, and from my soul lift the fear." On broken clay tablets, the anguish of a Hittite king has survived through the centuries.

The next king was Muwatallis (1306-1282 B.C.) who bested the flamboyant Egyptian, Ramses II, on the field of Kadesh. Muwatallis bequeathed to his son Urhi-Teshub a relatively stable and prosperous empire. But Muwatallis was also survived by his able and ambitious brother Hattusilis, who controlled the northeastern

63

part of the empire virtually as an independent kingdom.

As to what happened next we only have Hattusilis III's account, for he overthrew Urhi-Teshub and losers rarely have a chance to leave behind their side of the story for history to evaluate. But the ease with which Hattusilis usurped the throne gives the distinct impression that Urhi-Teshub was less than popular with his subjects, and the account probably contains a good deal of truth.

In his "autobiography" or, more properly, his justification for rebellion Hattusilis tells how as a child he suffered from ill health. (This complaint can be found in the records of other Hittite kings and it is clear they made no claims to superhuman powers.) He also says he was always surrounded by jealous enemies, and that after his brother's death the new king joined the ranks of his enemies. "But out of respect for my brother, I loyally did not act selfishly and for seven years I complied. But then that man sought to destroy me. . . ." (Urhi-Teshub took away some of his land) "and then I complied no more but revolted from him." Hattusilis says he made no secret of his intentions. "I [openly] declared war on him [saying]: 'You picked a quarrel with me. . . .' "

If anyone cared to question the justice of his revolt Hattusilis had a ready reply: "Would [the gods] have made him, a great king, lose to a petty king? But because now he has picked a quarrel with me, the gods by their verdict would have made him lose to me. . . ." Today this sounds like a weak excuse, but it would not have sounded so to the Hittites who believed the gods caused the just side to prevail in the "ordeal" of battle.

Hattusilis banished Urhi-Teshub and his followers, a decision he may, at times, have regretted. The former king was sent into exile in Nuhassi, a distant Syrian province of the empire. His life in Nuhassi was clearly not too restricted, for a few years later we hear of him again. Hattusilis' annals note that Urhi-Teshub was intriguing with the king of Babylon. So the banished ruler was taken from Nuhassi and sent "aside to the sea." The meaning of the phrase is

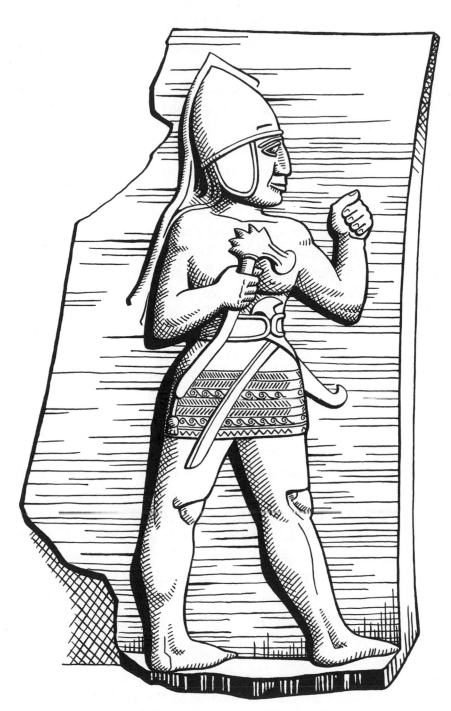

Relief of Hittite god from Boghazköy

not clear, but it may indicate that his place of exile was removed to the island of Cyprus. Still, Urhi-Teshub could not remain quiet, for further records note that he approached the king of Egypt. However, there is no hint that any of the foreign monarchs were rash enough to give him any aid in his quest to regain the throne.

When Hattusilis led his rebellion in 1289 B.C. he was a man of nearly fifty and a seasoned war leader. Yet further conquest did not seem to interest him. The fragmentary remains of Hattusilis' archives tell of some military operations undertaken in the west to shore up the borders of the empire but, in the main, the reign of Hattusilis III seems to have been one of peace and prosperity. A large number of dedications of temples and public buildings bearing the seal of Hattusilis III have been found and it is reasonable to assume that extensive public works projects were constructed under his direction. Relations between the Hittites and Ramses II of Egypt which may have been strained at first—a letter from the king of Babylon promised Hattusilis aid in the event of a war with Egypt—grew increasingly friendly, until they concluded their famous peace treaty of 1284 B.C.

In 1906 Hugo Winckler, director of the German expedition at Boghazköy, sat in his mud hut tediously deciphering bits of clay tablets that his expedition had been turning up by the thousands. An aging and terribly ill man, with only a few years left to live, Winckler had been pushed into a state of apathy by pain. Then came the find that gave him new life. "On Aug. 20," he wrote, "after some twenty days of digging . . . a beautifully preserved tablet was found, which even in its outward appearance looked promising. I glanced at it— and all my previous experiences vanished into nothingness. Here it was, the very thing I might perhaps jestingly have longed for as a pious wish."

The treaty between Ramses II and the Hittites was well known because Ramses had a monumental version of it carved into the walls of his temple at Karnak. The importance of the treaty had escaped the scholars because the Pharaoh had preceded it with such elaborate self-glorification that it sounded as though he were making an agreement with a minor tribal chief. What Winckler, 1,200 miles away from Karnak, held in his hands was the Hittite version of the very same treaty which had miraculously survived after more than 3,100 years. This find established two things. First, it firmly linked the mysterious mountain people of Asia Minor to the Hittites known from the Egyptian records and monuments (and indirectly to the Hittites of the Bible). Second, it proved that the ground Winckler was excavating was the Hittite capital itself, for it was obviously the storehouse of royal records.

The peace treaty proved popular with both sides and communication between the two countries became increasingly frequent. We even possess a letter from Hattusilis' queen, Puduhepa, to the queen of Egypt, apparently part of an independent correspondence the two queens engaged in. Hittite queens seemed to occupy a position of unusual importance in society. This was particularly true of Puduhepa, whom Hattusilis had married rather late in his life. Her name was regularly associated with that of her husband in state documents, and the treaty with Egypt contains not only the king's seal but Puduhepa's private seal as well.

Fourteen years later the friendship between the two nations was cemented by a marriage between a daughter of Hattusilis III and Puduhepa, and Ramses II. Egyptian records (our best source for this event) describe the marriage in such a way as to give all the glory to Ramses, but it is interesting to note that the Hittite princess had soon maneuvered her way to the top position in the Pharaoh's extensive harem.

Hattusilis III must have died shortly after the royal marriage was concluded, for by that time he was nearly seventy. With his passing the peak of Hittite power also passed and under his successors, Tudhaliyas IV, Arnuwandas IV, and Suppiluliumas II, the empire began a decline, so rapid that many have found it bewildering. Within two generations the Hittites had been entirely overrun and the capital sacked and burned. Excavations show that the ruins must have smoldered for days and weeks afterward. The destruction was complete. Although towns and villages were built near the site, the mountain stronghold of the Hittites never again played an important part in history.

Records from this final period of Hittite history are scarce, so the reasons for the overthrow of the empire are unknown, but it seems to be related to vast migrations of peoples that were taking place throughout the ancient world. Even the Egyptians in their geographically protected land felt the power of these mass movements. Invaders they called the Peoples of the Sea battered Egyptian armies again and again. Isolation saved the Egyptians, but on the walls of the temple of Medinet Habu we find this line in a description of the invasion by the Peoples of the Sea: "And no land held fast before them—from the land of Hatti down!"

The empire was gone, but Hittite influence lingered for centuries. Hittite customs hung on in city states which had once been part of the empire, and Hittite hieroglyphic symbols have been found dating from as late as the first century A.D. When the Assyrian conquerors swept through the former Hittite domain they encountered several self-styled "Great Kings of Hatti." These were nothing more than the rulers of petty states who were trying to recapture lost grandeur.

Ironically, it is because Boghazköy was burned to the ground that we know so much about the Hittites today. The British archaeologist, Sir Leonard Woolley, has said: "If the field archaeologist had his will, every ancient capital would have been overwhelmed by the ashes of a conveniently adjacent volcano. Failing a volcano, the best thing that can happen to a city, archaeologically speaking, is that it should be sacked and very thoroughly burnt by an enemy."

Sudden, violent destruction freezes a city in a moment of time. The richest archaeological sites in the world are the Roman cities of

Hittite animal relief

Pompeii and Herculaneum, destroyed by an eruption of Mount Vesuvius. At Boghazköy the fire baked clay tablets to rock hardness. The buildings were burned, but the foundations remained. Under the ashes the ruins were safe from the insidious corrosion of time and the meddling hands of man. They remained undisturbed until they were carefully dug out by archaeologists.

Enough is known to attempt at least a brief assessment of the importance of the Hittites. Much of it must be negative. They left behind no real literature. Hittite art displays a certain crude power, but it is generally stumpy and unattractive. Hittite architecture is massive, but neither attractive nor particularly functional, although this is an area that needs much more study. At one time it was thought that the Hittites invented the war chariot, and it was because of it that they attained their power. Certainly the Hittites were superlative charioteers, perhaps the best in the ancient world, but they did not invent the chariot, and they even had to import foreigners to train their chariot horses.

The Hittites knew iron very early, and there has been a good deal of speculation that Hittite power rested on use of iron weapons —far better than the bronze and stone weapons common at the time

69

—and a monopoly of iron, for the mountains of Asia Minor are rich in iron ore. There are letters from Egyptian kings begging for iron, and Hattusilis III wrote to the King of Assyria: "As for the good iron which you wrote about to me, good iron is not available in my seal-house in Kizzuwatna. That it is a bad time for producing iron I have written. They will produce good iron, but as yet they will not have finished. When they have finished I shall send it to you. Today, now I am dispatching an iron dagger-blade to you." This passage gives a glimpse into the commercial relations between the kingdoms, but too many conclusions cannot be drawn from it. To the Hittites, iron was used as an ormental metal, more expensive than gold. An iron-bladed dagger would have been a ceremonial object, not a weapon. Iron weapons were probably introduced by the Peoples of the Sea who used them to overthrow the Hittites.

The accomplishments of the Hittites, and the reasons for their rise to power, lie almost purely in their mastery of politics. It is the character and intelligence of kings like Hattusilis III, not chariots or iron swords, that forged the empire. The Hittites were never a large unified culture; rather they were a small elite who possessed the ability and will to dominate and lead the heterogeneous tribes around them. With a clear-eyed view of political realities, and fully conscious of their own abilities and limitations, they became what the archaeological writer C. W. Ceram has called "the most splendid and amazing political phenomenon of ancient history."

Is that all? Were they just a phenomenon contributing little if anything to the mainstream of world history? There are hints, at present nothing more, that the Hittites, in some unknown way gave some of their social- and self-awareness to the early Greeks. If this proves to be true, the entire question of the Hittites' importance to the development of European civilization will have to be re-evaluated.

CHAPTER FIVE

MINOS

Legend Come to Life

ANCIENT GREEK MYTHS have a great deal to say about the island of Crete and its legendary ruler King Minos. Crete is a large island in the Aegean Sea, sixty miles southeast of the Greek mainland. During classical times—that period of Greek history that is well known to us—the island did not play a very important role. But the classical Greeks believed that Zeus, their chief god, was born in a cave on Mount Ida in Crete.

Later, Zeus, in his wanderings about the earth, was attracted by the beauty of the young Europa, daughter of the King of Phoenicia. The god changed himself into the form of a gentle bull, and induced the trusting Europa to climb onto his back. Suddenly the great beast was docile no longer. It sprang into the water and carried Europa off to Crete.

There were three children from the union of the god and the mortal girl: Minos, Rhadamanthys, and Sarpedon. All three were adopted by the King of Crete, Asterius, who subsequently became Europa's husband. When Asterius died, Minos became king of Crete.

The image of the bull comes back again in the story of Minos. The king's wife Pasiphae bore a half-human, half-bull monster

71

called the Minotaur. This monster lived exclusively on human flesh, and Minos kept it imprisoned in the labyrinth, a fantastic structure with so many rooms and corridors that it was impossible to find a way out.

Minos' fleet ruled a great sea empire, and the mighty king had a particular quarrel with the city of Athens. He imposed a cruel tribute on the Athenians. Each year he took seven of the city's youths and seven maidens to Crete and threw them into the labyrinth to be devoured by the Minotaur. This ghastly practice went on for three years until the Athenian hero Theseus determined to bring an end to his city's servitude. As the seven unfortunate young men were being picked by Minos' emissaries, Theseus stepped forward and volunteered to become part of the tribute. Like many Greek heroes, Theseus was extremely handsome and irresistible to women. Once on Crete, Ariadne, Minos' daughter, fell in love with the Athenian, and with her aid he was able to get into the labyrinth, kill the monster in a furious battle, and find his way out again.

The labyrinth was constructed by Daedalus, probably the most intriguing character in the tangle of legends that surround Minos and Crete. Daedalus, so the legend goes, was an Athenian craftsman and inventor of great genius and evil temper. He was forced to flee his homeland after killing a rival craftsman in a fit of jealousy. Minos gave him refuge and Daedalus built many wonderful things for the king. He is credited, for example, with the invention of the ax and the saw. When Ariadne was trying to save her lover Theseus, she knew that Daedalus, builder of the inescapable labyrinth, was the only man who could devise a way out of it. The great inventor's solution was amazingly simple. He told Ariadne to give Theseus a ball of wool which he was to unravel as he entered the labyrinth. After killing the Minotaur, Theseus had only to follow the wool to find his way out.

Minos knew that no one except Daedalus was clever enough to be responsible for Theseus' escape, so he had the inventor and his son Icarus imprisoned in the labyrinth. For a genius like Daedalus, this was only a momentary inconvenience. He fashioned wings of wax and the two prisoners flew to freedom. Icarus, however, grew rash, and flew too close to the sun. His wax wings melted and he plunged to his death in the sea. Daedalus was more careful and flew on to Sicily where he quickly became a favorite of the king there.

Minos then began a frantic search for his missing inventor, but was unable to locate him. So he cunningly baited a trap. Minos fashioned an intricately spiraled shell, and announced that he would give a rich reward to anyone who could pass a thread through the shell. Minos knew that such a challenge would be an overwhelming temptation to the egotistical inventor. And so it was. Daedalus sent for the shell, bored a small hole in one end of it, attached a thread to an ant, and put the ant into the shell. When the ant crawled out the other end, the thread had been pulled through all the twists and turns of the shell. "Only Daedalus would think of that," Minos said, and he came to Sicily to seize him. But the king of Sicily would not surrender his prize, and he had Minos treacherously killed in a trick bath built, of course, by Daedalus.

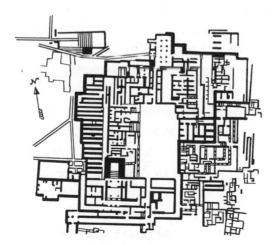

Floor plan of the labyrinth or "Palace of Minos" at Knossos

There are many variations of the legends of Crete, some of them quite contradictory. On the one hand, Minos is pictured as a terrible tyrant. Yet other legends portray him as a wise lawgiver, whose sense of justice earned him the position of Judge of the Underworld after his death.

A collection of wonderful but purely fanciful tales was the almost unanimous judgment of the scholars about the life of Minos. Imagine their surprise when archaeologists digging on Crete began to find things that showed, in the most incredible way, that the story of Minos was much more than a legend.

In 1871 Heinrich Schliemann, a rich German businessman, began a search for the ancient city of Troy. Troy was known only through the *Iliad* and the *Odyssey*, epic poems of the great Greek poet Homer. Most historians did not believe that a real city of Troy had ever existed. Schliemann, however, was no scholar; he had a simple and passionate faith in the literal truth of Homer. Following the *Iliad*, almost like a road map, he found Troy, much to the dismay of the professionals who were quite convinced that the wealthy eccentric was throwing his money away. Still following Homer, Schliemann went on to excavate Mycenae, on the Greek mainland, another city mentioned in the epics. Homer had spoken of "Golden Mycenae," so Schliemann was not in the least surprised when he found golden masks in the graves at Mycenae. There he also found inscribed stones and other curious objects of ancient origin. These were very similar to objects that had been found all around the Aegean, especially on the island of Crete. Homer had also written of Crete. In the *Iliad* Crete is mentioned as another Greek kingdom, so Schliemann determined to conduct excavations at Crete. The spot he chose was near the village of Knossos, an area known to be rich in ruins. But a dispute with the owner of the land arose, and Schliemann dropped the whole project in disgust. A year later he died. By inches he had missed what would have undoubtedly been the crowning discovery of his fantastic career.

Arthur Evans, the man who ultimately did uncover the secrets of Knossos, was a very different sort of man. An Englishman, Evans was the scholarly son of a scholar and interested in languages, not legends. He became intrigued by what seemed to be the Cretan origin of certain hieroglyphics. Evans visited Crete for the first time in 1894, when he was forty-three years old. In the beginning he assumed that he would be able to finish his business in Crete in a few months, a year at the most. A quarter century later he was digging in the same place. The uncovering of the civilization at Crete remained his ruling passion for the rest of his life, and he lived to be ninety-two. Evans also invested a good deal of his own personal fortune in reconstructing the ruins he had uncovered.

Almost immediately after he began excavations the remains of a vast sprawling palace were unearthed. The building had contained such a profusion of rooms, corridors, courtyards, and levels laid out in a pattern that seemed entirely random that it must have been a very easy place to get lost in. Even to Evans' coldly scientific mind, the word "labyrinth," home of the terrifying Minotaur, sprang to mind.

The symbol of the bull which occurs so frequently in the story of Minos was found everywhere. Most striking are those representations called the bull dancers. Painted on the walls and inscribed on stones are scenes of young men and women leaping over the backs of gigantic bulls. Although the human figures in these scenes seem to be dancers or acrobats, they are still strongly reminiscent of the story of the young Greeks thrown to the bull-headed monster.

Evans did not see these bull-leaping scenes as evidence of human sacrifice. He wrote: "The youthful participants in these performances—like those of the boxing and wrestling bouts, that can hardly be separated from the same general category—have certainly no servile appearance. . . . In these champions of either sex we must rather recognize the flower of the Minoan race, executing, in many cases under a direct religious sanction, feats of bravery and skill in

75

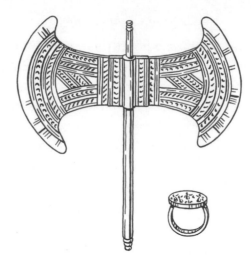

Gold model of double-ax and a Minoan seal ring

which the whole population took a passionate delight."

The handiwork of Daedalus, that master craftsman, seemed everywhere in evidence. The palace of Knossos contained a drainage system, luxurious bathrooms, and ventilation systems, far better than anything known until very modern times. There were also trick jugs, toys, and other impractical but extremely clever gadgetry. The most persistent symbol in the ruins was the double-headed ax, another of Daedalus' inventions, according to the myths.

During its height Crete had been wealthy and luxurious, just as the legends had said. A great part of the palace at Knossos was given over to storerooms, in which vast quantities of produce were kept. Also, as the legends had indicated, the wealth seemed to be based on mastery of the sea, rather than farming or warfare. Unlike most ancient cities, those on Crete have no walls. They needed none. The island could only be invaded from the sea, and in that realm the Cretans had no equals.

Small wonder that Evans reached back to the Greek legends and called his new-found civilization Minoan. But the most astounding thing Evans found was the great age of Minoan civilization. He dated its beginning at around 3000 B.C. and he believed it continued to flourish until 1400 B.C. when it was suddenly and violently destroyed. Without doubt it was the earliest known European civilization. Again there are echoes of the legends of Zeus, father of the gods, who was born on Crete, and the girl Europa, from whose name the word Europe comes.

At what point in this long history does the great King Minos come in? Unfortunately, we simply don't know. Minos' name has never been found in the ruins at Crete nor, for that matter, has any other name or anything resembling a royal inscription. The Minoans possessed a system of writing. Evans identified two forms of script which he called Linear A and Linear B. Language was his first interest and he optimistically assumed that he would quickly be able to decipher the Minoan scripts, but he never did.

In 1936 Evans delivered a lecture on Minoan civilization in London. In the audience was a fourteen-year-old schoolboy, Michael Ventris, who had already shown an unusual interest and talent for deciphering ancient languages. By the age of seven Ventris had studied Egyptian hieroglyphics. Listening to the grand old man of Minoan archaeology, the boy vowed to take up the puzzle of the scripts. He was educated as an architect but he never gave up his interest in languages. Sixteen years after hearing Evans, Ventris did what many had begun to think was impossible—he deciphered Linear B. Shortly after his triumph Ventris was tragically killed in an automobile accident.

Evans believed that the orderly Minoan tablets contained the famous laws of Minos. If they had, we would know a great deal more about the Minoans than we do. More optimistic scholars hoped that the tablets would shed some light on the stories in the Greek myths, perhaps reveal a Minoan Homer. These hopes were not fulfilled. Nor have there been any "king lists" common in other ancient societies or anything else that would help us reconstruct the history of Crete. The neat Linear B inscriptions have turned out to be lists of objects in the royal storerooms. For all their beautiful painting and architecture the people of Crete, it seems, were a practical lot, more interested in business than poetry. The origins of Linear B, however, did both illuminate and confuse the picture of Minoan civilization as Evans had reconstructed it.

Even without the help of Linear B, it is clear that the legend of Minos has a firm basis in historical fact. Minos himself may have been a single monarch, or an entire dynasty, or the word Minos may simply have meant king. Most modern scholars hold the view that Minos was a real individual or, at most, two kings with the same name. The Greeks, when recalling their contacts with the cultured people of Crete in the dim past, might easily have attributed the deeds of many rulers to a single great one. The Minoans lived in what must have seemed a stable, well-ordered society, a tremendous contrast to the rough and wild existence of the early Greeks; hence, the concept of Minos the lawgiver. Perhaps the Minoans worshipped bulls, or practiced some sort of ritual involving bulls. This was transformed into the story of the Minotaur. The technical accomplishments of the people of Crete surely were enormously impressive to people at a lower stage of development. These accomplishments were credited to the genius of a single man, Daedalus. But in order not to give all credit to a foreigner, the Greeks made Daedalus an Athenian.

Evans was so taken by the splendor of the Minoans that the attitude of the later Greeks annoyed him. He wrote: "It was, however, reserved for Athenian chauvinism so to exaggerate the tyrannical side of that early sea-domination as to convert the palace of a long series of great rulers into an ogre's den. But the fabulous accounts of the Minotaur and his victims are themselves expressive of a childish wonder at the mighty creations of a civilization beyond the ken of the new-comers. . . . The spade of the excavator had indeed done much to explain and confute them. The ogre's den turns out to be a peaceful abode of priest-kings, in some respects more modern in its equipment than anything produced by classical

The "bull dancers" fresco

Greece. . . . Minos 'the destroyer' may certainly have existed. That the yoke of the more civilized ruler should at times have weighed heavily on subject peoples is probable enough. But, in the main, the result of recent discovery has been to confirm the more favorable side of Greek tradition."

Many who have visited the ruins of Crete, or the reconstructions of the palace of Minos at Knossos, or even seen Minoan art in museums or books, have fallen under their spell, just as Evans did. These strange people of Crete covered their walls with paintings of slim, graceful figures or fantastic animals and plants on backgrounds of wildly colorful abstract designs. There is nothing quite like it in the ancient world—no wars, no battle scenes, no homages to the king, none of the traditional themes of the art of ancient civilizations. A minority of scholars have not fallen in love with Minoan art; rather they have been repelled by it. They believe it declined into an empty showiness, and indicated the decadence and weakness of the people who produced it.

Evans used the word "modern" to describe what he saw, yet without doubt Minoan civilization was very ancient. Where had it come from? Homer indicates that there were five different groups on Crete. The early Greek historian, Herodotus, says Minos was not

79

Greek, while another Greek historian, Thucydides, says he was. Obviously, the Greeks had forgotten a great deal about their contacts with the island civilization.

Minoan paintings indicate that the people of Crete were of a different racial type than the Greeks. A study of skeletons found on Crete seemed to confirm this. Evans held that the civilized Minoans were probably native to the island, descendants of peoples who had lived there since prehistoric times. The flowering of Minoan civilization came from two factors. First, the Minoans themselves were a talented and original people. Second, they were excellent sailors and traders, and this mode of life brought them into frequent contact with other civilizations of the Near East. They borrowed freely from the accomplishments of the peoples of Egypt, Mesopotamia, and Asia Minor. Evans thought that the major impulse for the rise of Minoan civilization came from Egypt, and even that refugees from early Egypt provided the skills that were needed to begin the high culture of Crete.

There is no doubt that there was a great deal of communication between Egypt and Crete. Egyptian pottery has been found in Minoan ruins and vice versa. Egyptian wall paintings show curiously garbed foreigners who are almost certainly visiting Minoans. But not all experts give so much credit to the influence of Egypt. Edward Dörpfeld, Schliemann's assistant and a noted professional archaeologist in his own right, contended that Minoan culture came directly from Phoenicia and did not develop in Crete at all. Dörpfeld could find a basis for his theory in the story of Europa; she had been a Phoenician.

Continuing excavations around Crete have made necessary revisions in many of the early theories. Scholars now think that civilization on Crete began very much later than Evans believed it had. They also assign more importance to the influence of such Asiatic people as the Hittites and less to Egypt. But, in general, they have not upset Evans' picture of the rise of Minoan civilization.

Figure of a young Minoan

A much more tantalizing question than the origins of Minoan civilization, which can probably never be clearly determined, is what happened to the Minoans? Suddenly, it seemed to Evans, around 1400 B.C. the "Palace of Minos" at Knossos and other Minoan buildings and palaces on Crete were destroyed, and the whole brilliant culture, which had for years dominated the Aegean, crumbled. All that was left were the ruins and the stories transmitted in a garbled way in the myths of the Greeks.

Evans, who had himself been caught in a violent earthquake on Crete, believed that just such a natural disaster, followed by social disorganization, brought an end to the power of Crete. Inevitably, others did not agree. They went back to the legend of Theseus and how he defeated the Minotaur. This, they felt, might have been a symbol for an invasion from the Greek mainland by people called Mycenaens, after the city of Mycenae, where Schliemann made his remarkable discoveries. Some supporters of the Mycenaen theory went even further. They saw the invasion from the mainland taking place long before the destruction of Crete, and they give the Mycenaen conquerors credit for the last brilliant period of the island's history. The destruction of Crete, they say, was due to an uprising by the native Minoans.

When Michael Ventris deciphered Linear B, it looked as though the arguments in favor of the mainlanders were right after all. According to Evans, the tablets had been written well before the fall of Knossos, but Ventris found Linear B was Greek, a very ancient and difficult form of Greek, to be sure, but definitely Greek. This put Greek-speaking people from the mainland in Crete long before Minoan civilization ended.

For most people the problem was solved, at least until 1962, when Professor Leonard Palmer, one of Ventris' associates, broke the controversy wide open once again. Palmer went back to Evans' original field notes and argued, very convincingly, that Evans had misdated the Linear B tablets. They were Greek, said Palmer, but they came from a much later period, perhaps as much as two hundred years after the date Evans assigned to the fall of Knossos.

In that case, Evans was wrong in his dating, but basically right in his theories. Not so, says Professor Palmer. Evans depicted the time after the destruction of Knossos as one of uninterrupted decay, but Palmer thinks that the palace was not really destroyed and deserted at all, and that the invaders set up a ruling dynasty that enjoyed two hundred years of prosperity and power, until they succumbed to another invasion from the mainland.

Recently archaeologists, oceanographers, and geologists have thrown new light on the possible cause of the fall of the Minoan empire. They have found evidence that around 1400 B.C. there occurred in the Aegean, near Crete, a tremendous volcanic explosion, one of the worst natural catastrophes in all history. At least one nearby island, Thera, partially sank, and some archaeologists believe this disaster inspired the Greek story of the lost continent of Atlantis. A Minoan town on Thera, buried in the ash and lava, has been uncovered, almost intact. This is one of the great archaeological finds of the century.

Ash from the explosion fell for fifty years, and the deposit is so thick in some places that it may have ruined Minoan agriculture and helped bring the civilization down.

Even with all the unanswered questions, the rediscovery of the fabulous civilization on the island of Crete has been a magnificent accomplishment. At the age of eighty-eight, Sir Arthur Evans summed it up this way: "We know now that the old traditions were true. We have before our eyes a wondrous spectacle. . . . It is true that on the old palace site what we see are only the ruins of ruins, but the whole is still inspired with Minos's spirit of order and organization, and the free and natural art of the great architect Daedalus."

CHAPTER SIX

SENNACHERIB

The Bloody Monarch

THE ASSYRIANS have a bad reputation and of all the fierce Assyrian kings, Sennacherib's reputation is the worst.

Assyria had a great empire and, like other empires, it was built and maintained by constant warfare. War is always cruel, but the Assyrians used terror as a deliberate instrument of policy, and they were very proud of it.

Sennacherib was no crueler than other Assyrian monarchs but he committed one act which must have shocked even the Assyrians; he destroyed the greatest city in the world—Babylon. Assyria had conquered Babylon many times but the people there were always restless and seized every chance for revolt. The kings of Assyria hated rebels, yet treated Babylon with unaccustomed mildness. Babylon's great size, age, and culture made it the most prized possession of the empire. In addition, the deeply religious Assyrians had proper respect for the ancient gods of Babylon, which were so like their own.

In 689 B.C. Babylon staged one of its frequent revolts. Allying herself with other Assyrian enemies, the combined armies came close to inflicting a humiliating defeat on Sennacherib. The king, frantic with rage, determined to clear rebellious Babylon from the face of the earth.

"As a hurricane proceeds, I attacked it and like a storm I overthrew it. . . . Its inhabitants, young and old I did not spare and with their corpses I filled the streets of the city. . . . The town itself and its houses from their foundations to their roofs I devastated, I destroyed, by fire I overthrew. . . . In order that, in future, even the soil of its temples be forgotten, by water I ravaged it, I turned it into pastures."

An unprecedented and dreadful act. In less than eight years the gods of Babylon seemed to take their revenge. In 681 B.C., while praying in a temple, Sennacherib was "smashed with statues of protective deities" by his own sons.

Sennacherib's reputation for destruction has almost obscured another side of the king's character. He was probably one of the most technically astute rulers of the ancient world. The feats of construction accomplished during his reign are magnificent. True, the real work was done by a highly trained corps of engineers, but so much was accomplished so quickly that it is reasonable to assume that the king kept a close and knowing eye on the work.

Even the technical feat involved in destroying Babylon inspires a sort of horrified admiration. Not content with merely burning the city to the ground, the enraged king had the river Euphrates damned, dug canals around the city, and sent the river waters flowing through them, turning Babylon into a mudhole.

Among the many peoples whom the Assyrians fought were the Hebrews. The Prophets declared openly what many must have hoped for:

> And it shall come to pass
> that all they that look upon thee
>   shall flee from thee,
> and say: Ninevah [Sennacherib's capital]
>   is laid waste: who will bemoan her?

Since the Assyrians had come into conflict with the Hebrews, their name has never been lost. But while the names of Assyrian cities are frequently mentioned in the Old Testament, their exact

Sennacherib

location is not recorded. For thousands of years no one knew where they were, and few cared.

The flat plain of Mesopotamia is dotted with mounds; they are odd looking, but there is nothing to indicate that they were not natural features of the landscape. Yet, according to the Old Testament, it was in this area that the Assyrians had flourished. Could great cities have disappeared without a trace? Some people suspected that their ruins lay beneath the mounds. One of those people was Paul Emile Botta, a young French physician and diplomat, stationed in the Middle East.

In 1840 he began poking around the mounds near the city of Mosul, on the upper Tigris, where he was consular agent. For a year he found little of interest. Then a local Arab told him of another mound where ancient things could be found just beneath the surface. Botta was curious enough to dispatch a small crew of diggers to the mound near the village of Khorsabad. Almost immediately they met with success, and a success so stunning that Botta himself could hardly believe it. In a short time he was able to write to Paris: "I believe that I am the first to discover sculptures that can be truly identified with the period when Ninevah was at its height."

At about the same time a youthful English romantic, Austen Henry Layard, was, in his own words, "wandering through Asia Minor and Syria, scarcely leaving untrod one spot hallowed by tradition, or unvisited one ruin consecrated by history. . . . I now felt an irresistible desire to penetrate to the regions beyond the Euphrates, to which history and tradition point as the birthplace of the wisdom of the West."

Like Botta, Layard was attracted by "a line of lofty mounds." By 1845 Layard had collected a small sum of money with which he planned to begin excavations of the mound that tradition identified with the Assyrian city of Nimrud. Layard's success was immediate, and even more striking than Botta's. His diggers unearthed over a dozen pairs of colossal stone winged bulls and lions. After a great deal of trouble Layard managed to send a smaller pair of the monumental monsters to London where an awe-struck public gazed for the first time on the alien-looking creations of an almost mythical people.

Layard's greatest triumph came five years later when he had moved his expedition to the mounds of Sennacherib's city of Ninevah. One of Sennacherib's successors, Ashurbanipal, had sent an army of scribes throughout his domain to copy all important documents. They took the copies back to the king, who added two rooms to his palace to hold them. The Assyrians, like the other people of ancient Mesopotamia, wrote on clay tablets. It was this library of sturdy clay writings that Layard uncovered at Ninevah.

Layard's find did not mark the first time that Europeans had seen cunieform inscriptions. Tablets had been found from time to time and the script had already been deciphered at the beginning of the nineteenth century. So the tablets in Ashurbanipal's library could be read quickly.

Many of them contained instructions for conducting magical rites, but there were also king lists, historical descriptions, and political edicts, as well as some literary works. As a result, within a very few years scholars were able to piece together a picture of Assyrian life and history far more complete than that possessed by the very peoples who overthrew the empire.

In the beginning the Assyrians were just one of the many tribes that lived in Mesopotamia. The nucleus of the Assyrian state formed around the northern city of Assur, named after the nation's chief god. Mesopotamia was always at war and the land of the Assyrians was particularly vulnerable to attack from nearby states and wandering nomads. Early in their history the Assyrians had to develop their fighting ability. They learned the arts of war well and Assyria evolved into a superb military machine.

A brief foreshadowing of later imperial glory was attained under Tiglathpileser I (1115-1077 B.C.). This monarch claimed to have conquered Babylon, all of Syria, and cities as far away as Phoenicia. The claim is exaggerted. Tiglathpileser may have fought successful battles in these distant lands but he did not secure his conquests. Tiglathpileser I suffered a fate common to Assyrian kings; he was murdered. Upon his death his fragile empire collapsed, while at home a power struggle plunged Assyria into a time of "troubles and disorders." For 166 years Assyria was in the dark ages. Records from the period are virtually nonexistent.

Only the confusion and weakness of her enemies saved Assyria from being conquered. With the accession of Adad-Nirari II in 911 B.C., the blackout of Assyrian history ended, and her greatest age began. Attacks by a formidable Assyrian army weakened any states which might have been contemplating aggression against Assyria.

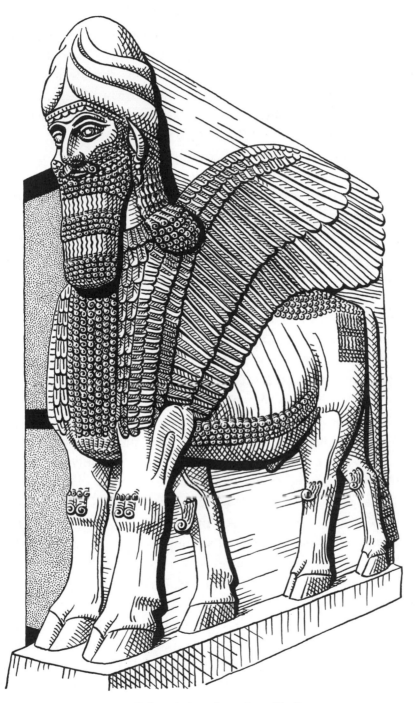

Colossal Assyrian winged bull

The Assyrians had been conquered many times in their early days and lived in mortal fear of this happening again. Their style of warfare may have had something of a religious crusade about it, and this may account for their recourse to terrorism. They were fanatically religious, and they regarded their enemies as enemies of their gods. The killing of "devils" is not a cruel act to the fanatic; it is not even an unfortunate political necessity, but a justifiable punishment. The grim fact is that holy wars are often the most terrible.

The first great monarch of the new period was Ashurnasirpal II (884-859 B.C.). He carried on his raids almost unopposed, and it is in his records that scholars found the most ghastly descriptions of Assyrian cruelty. "It is difficult to say," writes the scholar George Roux, "which is more shocking: the atrocities themselves, or the detailed methodical, self-gratifying way in which the chief executioner describes them."

Ashurnasirpal's son, Shalmaneser III, was even more warlike than his father, spending thirty-one of his thirty-five years of reign at war. Ashurnasirpal had declined to conquer Babylon, although he could have done so. When in 851 B.C. a revolt broke out in Babylon, Shalmaneser intervened on the side of the legitimate king. He entered Babylon and, rather than sacking the city, treated the residents to a great feast and "clothed them in brightly coloured garments and presented them with gifts."

Near the end of Shalmaneser's reign, however, family dissension, the curse of Assyrian royalty, broke out and lasted until another powerful and vigorous sovereign took the throne in 745 B.C. Tiglathpileser III determined to end the confusion in his kingdom by initiating a number of drastic reforms which basically changed the nature of the Assyrian state.

What Tiglathpileser did was to increase royal authority and reduce the power of the great Assyrian barons and the princes of the subject states. Previous monarchs had been content to allow cooperative local rulers to remain on their thrones, so long as they paid a regular tribute to Assyria. Tiglathpileser believed this system encouraged revolt and, wherever practical, he removed native rulers and replaced them with Assyrian governors under his direct control. Where this could not be done the prince was assigned an Assyrian official to guide him and watch him like a hawk. Roads and communication were improved enormously, and news could be quickly conveyed to the king.

Babylon was again troublesome, and Tiglathpileser attempted to end the problem once and for all. He defeated the rebellious monarch who had taken the throne and had himself proclaimed king of Babylon.

Tiglathpileser III died in 726 B.C. and one of his sons reigned briefly before another great monarch came to the Assyrian throne. It is unknown whether this king was a usurper or another of Tiglathpileser's sons. He was called Sargon II.

Sargon, too, had a passion for building. He constructed a great new city for himself at Dur-Sharrukin, but he was killed in battle just a year after it was finished and the scarcely inhabited city was quickly deserted and fell into ruin.

Sennacherib was not Sargon's oldest son—his name means "the God Sin has increased the number of his brothers"—but he had been chosen legitimate heir and was well trained for the kingship before the unexpected death of his royal father.

The Jews of Palestine had been extremely troublesome to Sargon and they were even more so to his son. Finally, in 701 B.C., Sennacherib attacked Judah and trapped king Ezekiah in Jerusalem. The situation seemed hopeless, but Ezekiah was inspired to resist by the prophet Isaiah and by the promise of Egyptian support. The Bible describes how the Assyrians mocked the Jews for relying upon "the staff of this bruised reed, Egypt." But Jerusalem held, and a compromise was finally reached, although it was a very expensive one for the Jews. Aside from paying a tremendous bribe to Sennacherib, several cities were taken from the kingdom of Judah.

Sennacherib's next move was to begin an invasion of Judah's promised ally, Egypt. But the plan came to a disastrous end. The Bible says an angel of the Lord ravaged the Assyrian camp. According to Herodotus, the Greek historian, there was a plague of rats which ate all the rope and leather in the Assyrian camp. Another Greek writer speaks of a pestilence that swept through the army. Assyrian records are silent on this event.

Babylon presented the Assyrians with a more formidable problem. Marduk-apal-iddina, one of Sargon's old enemies who had been driven into exile, returned and captured Babylon. He was

defeated by the Assyrians but, with his followers, fled to the swamps "where he could not be found." As the new king of Babylon, Sennacherib appointed a young Babylonian who had grown up in Assyria and was thought to be trustworthy. But as soon as the Assyrian troops withdrew, the plotting began and Sennacherib was forced to return and put his own son, Ashur-nadin-shumi, on the throne.

A few years later Sennacherib launched an elaborate land and sea offensive aimed at giving the Assyrians access to the Persian Gulf and, incidentally, to seek out Marduk-apal-iddina and his

The Assyrian army besieges a fortified town

followers who were still hiding in the swamps of the lower Tigris. In planning the operation the king called upon skills developed in far-flung parts of his empire. A fleet of ships was built at Ninevah by craftsmen from Syria. Phoenicians and Cypriots, representatives of great seafaring races, provided the crews. But it was the technical genius of the Assyrians and their king that provided the key to the unusual attack. The ships were floated down the Tigris until the river became impassable. Then they were partially dismantled and carried overland to the Euphrates, where they picked up troops from the Assyrian army and conveyed them down to the mouth of the river in much less time than it would have taken to march the distance. The campaign was extremely successful because Assyria's enemies were not expecting a swift attack from the river.

These raids had been conducted in the land of the Elamites, who revenged themselves by encouraging another revolt in ever-restive Babylon. It was at this point that Sennacherib made his fateful decision to destroy the ancient city.

Assyrian kings loved to build royal cities for themselves. Sennacherib was no exception. He abandoned his father's just-completed capital and moved to Ninevah which he completely rebuilt and enlarged. The pride of the new royal capital was the king's huge gardens in which pet lions roamed. Keeping these gardens watered in bone-dry Mesopotamia was a task of great difficulty in which Sennacherib participated enthusiastically. He is said to have personally invented a new type of irrigation bucket, and to have chosen the sites for irrigation canals. As the royal gardens and forests grew in extent, water had to be brought from greater and greater distances.

One of Sennacherib's most prized accomplishments was a great canal and aqueduct which brought water to Ninevah from a distance of thirty miles. The king himself was to order the opening of the sluice gates of the canal. But before he could arrive on the scene one of the gates gave way and the water poured down the canal without awaiting the royal command. To the superstitious

An Assyrian king in his state chariot

Assyrians this was a powerful omen. But how was it to be interpreted? Sennacherib decided to take a cheerful view and declared that the gods had been so anxious to see the new waterworks in operation that they caused the gate to give way.

He wrote, "Those men who had dug that canal I clothed with linen and brightly colored woolen garments. Golden rings, daggers of gold I put upon them." The workmen were doubtless overjoyed that their royal master was in such a good mood, for he would have been perfectly capable of having them executed.

Sennacherib did not survive long enough to truly enjoy his accomplishments. His murder by his sons in 681 B.C. brought a sudden but not unexpected end to his violent life. One of the sons,

Esarhaddon, emerged victor from the short but bloody struggle that followed Sennacherib's death. Esarhaddon had been chosen as legitimate successor, but he had not always stood high in his father's favor. He declared that slanderous accusations by his brothers had turned his father against him, and that he had been forced to flee the country. Whether or not he took part in the plot to kill Sennacherib is not known, but he claimed that the other sons "butted each other like kids to take over the kingship." Esarhaddon raised an army and marched on Assyria. According to his records the soldiers of his brothers quickly deserted to his side and the people rushed to kiss his feet. His rebellious brothers fled, but Esarhaddon took no chances and had them hunted down and killed, along with their entire families.

Perhaps Esarhaddon thought his father's death was the punishment laid upon him by the gods for destroying Babylon, and he hastened to atone for the sin by rebuilding the city. Sennacherib had said that Babylon should lie in ruins for seventy years, but Esarhaddon's priests declared, "The merciful Marduk [chief god of Babylon] turned the Book of Fate upside down and ordered the restoration of the city in the eleventh year." (In cunieform, 70 becomes 11 when turned upside down.)

Esarhaddon's son Ashurbanipal was able to take power without incident upon his father's death. Ashurbanipal is without doubt the best liked of the Assyrian kings. Certainly he has earned the gratitude of generations of scholars for collecting his magnificent library. But he was, in reality, no less warlike than his ancestors, although most of his efforts were turned toward suppressing revolts rather than conquering new territories.

Ashurbanipal's empire looked like the strongest state in the world, but the appearance was deceptive. The land and its people were exhausted by constant warfare and internal factionalism. The army was no longer made up of native Assyrians, but consisted largely of less vigorous and less trustworthy foreign troops. New states and people had risen and gathered strength and they waited eagerly for the first sign of Assyrian weakness. They did not have to wait long.

In 639 B.C., eight years before his death, Ashurbanipal's extensive records abruptly and mysteriously cease. Perhaps the reason for the silence was civil disorder, or perhaps the silence was due to increasing attacks from the outside.

A few shadowy monarchs ruled after Ashurbanipal's death, but little is known of them. The final assault was led by Babylon, once again independent, and the distant Medes and Persians. Scholars have discovered Babylonian chronicles beginning in the year 626 B.C. which describe, in detail, the decline of the Assyrian empire from that date onward.

Assyria's epitaph was written in 612 B.C. by the Babylonian king Nabopolassar:

"I slaughtered the land of Assyria, I turned the hostile land to heaps and ruins."

As the Hebrew prophets had predicted, no one lamented the fall of Sennacherib's Ninevah.

CHAPTER SEVEN

CH'IN SHIH HUANG TI

The Most Powerful Man in History

CH'IN SHIH HUANG TI, the "First Emperor" of China, was probably the most powerful man who ever lived. Yet in the West he is practically unknown. All the surviving accounts of his life were written by his enemies. Some of the events sound so fantastic they are hard to believe. The First Emperor built the Great Wall of China, and a tomb which may have made the pyramids of Egypt look puny. But there has never been a great deal of archaeological exploration in China, so many of his feats cannot be verified. We don't even really know what he looked like, for only one likeness of the Emperor survives from his time. It is a poorly carved figure on a stone tomb, and shows him running from an assassination attempt, one of the least glorious episodes of his life. Ch'in Shih Huang Ti seems mythical as Zeus and as evil as Lucifer, yet he lived.

We shall try to separate fact from legend, with particular stress on those events that are supported by archaeological record, in building a portrait of this truly extraordinary man.

China possesses the oldest continuous culture of any existing nation. Indeed, Chinese civilization has lasted longer than any other in history except that of Egypt. Compared to the ancient civilizations of the Middle East, China developed slowly and late.

98

Archaeologists have found evidence of primitive, though well-established, settlements in the valley of the Yellow River as early as 4000 B.C. Around 2000 B.C. China seems to have undergone a population explosion. Thousands of villages appear for the first time.

The Chinese called their first rulers the Three August Ones. They were followed by the Five Sovereigns. According to legends their time was a golden age. Sometime at the beginning of the second millenium B.C. the first known dynasty, the Hsia, came to power. The stories of the Hsia sound reasonable, although there is not a scrap of archaeological proof to indicate that they were ever reality.

The Hsia were overthrown, according to tradition, in 1523 B.C. by the Shangs. Here, solid archaeological record begins to bring the blurred picture into focus. The existence of the Shangs was not established until the late 1920's. Shang artifacts had been collected for hundreds of years, but no one knew what they were.

In 1079 there was a terrific storm in the northern Chinese city of Anyang. The tempest tore open a huge mound near the city and when the astonished residents entered they found it had been a tomb. Among the bones they discovered beautifully worked bronze vessels, which were quickly sold to rich Chinese art lovers. As the demand grew, the people of Anyang began to dig up other mounds and finally to make their own bronzes. It was not until 1927 that systematic excavation of the source of the wonderful bronzes began. The people of Anyang greeted archaeologists with open hostility, for they felt that scientific exploration would bring an end to the thriving local industry of tomb robbing and the manufacture of fake antiquities. Archaeological excavations were extremely difficult, but worth the trouble; the mounds at Anyang had covered the tombs of the almost mythical Shangs.

There is a pattern in Chinese history in which vigorous warlike people sweep down and conquer the soft-living farmers, but are quickly seduced by the luxury and themselves become decadent and soft, easy prey for the next wave of hardy invaders. This happened

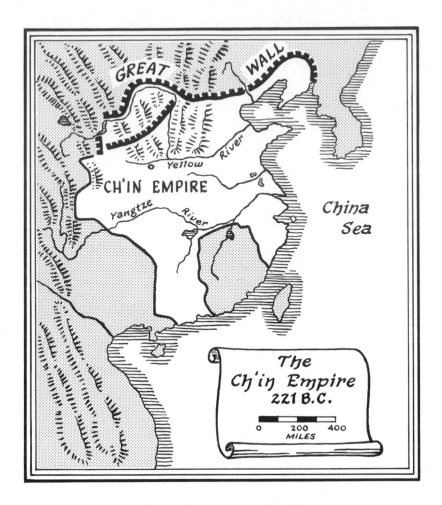

The Ch'in Empire 221 B.C.

to the Shangs when they fell victim to the Chou.

The Chou had a king, but the land was divided into provinces, each ruled by a powerful noble. As time went on these nobles became more and more independent. The king was reduced from the position of a political leader to that of a spiritual leader and even this power slipped away. China splintered into petty states that waged constant war on one another. The Chinese call this "the Era of the Contending States."

The time of wall building began. First, the nobles built walls to protect their cities, and finally much larger walls to protect their entire territory. The names of the states—Ch'in, Ch'i, Yen, Lu—are confusing, but for now only one name needs to be remembered. It is that of Ch'in.

Ch'in was the easternmost of the states. Territorially it was small and culturally it was backward, even barbaric. Most of the Chinese regarded the people of Ch'in as little better than the wild nomads. But they could not feel superior to the military might of Ch'in. Time after time the armies of Ch'in defeated those of other states.

Warfare during the Era of the Contending States was not the struggle to the death business it was to become later. Even the savage men of Ch'in obeyed the elaborate ritual which surrounded defeat and victory. Of course, it was not all a game; many people were killed. But when the battle was over the defeated lord would acknowledge his defeat, agree to pay a tribute, and be allowed to retain his land and privileges, not to mention his life. Ch'in Shih Huang Ti was to change all of that. Even before the "First Emperor" came to the throne, the state of Ch'in began a new policy by annexing the small state of Chou in 256 B.C. and ending the fiction that the King of Chou ruled China.

Much of our information about the Emperor Ch'in Shih Huang Ti comes from the account of Ssu-ma Ch'ien, Grand Historian of China, written about a century after the Emperor's death. The Grand Historian's patrons were descendants of the man who overthrew the empire of Ch'in and it is to be expected that he would draw an unflattering portrait.

Ssu-ma Ch'ien described the emperor thus: "High-pointed nose, slit eyes, pigeon breast, wolf voice, tiger heart, stingy, cringing, graceless." He says that the Emperor was not even of royal blood, but that he was the illegitimate son of a merchant named Lu Pu-wei who tricked the King of Ch'in into thinking the child was his own. It is safe to conclude that this is a slanderous invention.

The future emperor's father, King Chuang-hsiang, died after

101

reigning only four years, and his thirteen-year-old son Prince Cheng came to the throne of Ch'in in 251 B.C. Later Cheng was to take the name, Ch'in Shih Huang Ti.

While the king was still a boy, the merchant Lu Pu-wei was his chief adviser and virtual ruler of Ch'in. But the merchant proved to be scheming and ambitious. (However, it must be recalled that this information comes from the accounts of writers who hated the merchant class.) In 238 B.C. Lu's activities touched off a revolt which the King crushed ruthlessly, even expelling his own mother from the kingdom. Shortly afterward he ordered his former adviser into exile. Because he could not face the dishonor, or perhaps because he feared a worse fate, Lu Pu-wei drank poison.

King Cheng's new adviser was Li Ssu, a scholar of humble origins. Li Ssu was not even a native of Ch'in, but early in life he decided that the future lay with that warlike state. His superior abilities allowed him to rise rapidly in the Ch'in civil service. With the king's former confidant dead, Li Ssu moved easily into the position of the second most powerful man in Ch'in.

There were two political philosophies current in China of the day. The oldest and most famous was based on the teachings of Confucius who probably lived around 551 to 479 B.C. Today Confucius is primarily known by a profusion of sayings beginning, "Confucius say . . ." Unfortunately, Confucius never said most of those things. In fact, we don't really know what he did say, for during his life he wrote nothing. His students gathered together a great body of ideas and attributed them all to his teachings. Since Confucius was a popular figure during most periods of Chinese history, practically everything has been attributed to him. In the early days the essence of Confucian philosophy was that rulers should lead by example. Kings should be "superior men" who lived in accordance with basic moral principles. The philosophy was profoundly conservative, laying great stress on respect for age, station in life, and tradition.

The only known contemporary likeness of Ch'in Shih Huang Ti

Some two hundred years after Confucius there rose another school of philosophy known as Legalism. The "superior man" did not exist for the Legalists. Wrote Hsun-tzu, founder of this school of thought, "benevolence, righteousness, love and favor are not worth adopting, while severe punishment and heavy penalties can maintain the State in order." Li Ssu was an ardent Legalist, and the most successful practitioner of that grim philosophy.

Immediately following the rise of Li Ssu the nature of Ch'in

Confucius

warfare changed dramatically. Now when King Cheng's armies won a victory they refused to abide by the traditional rules of warfare. Ch'in simply gobbled up the defeated state. By 221 B.C. all the old contending states were under the domination of Ch'in. King Cheng showed no Confucian respect for the position of the defeated kings. They were "subjected to all the penalties befitting their crimes." The whole ancient and elaborate feudal nobility was swept away.

The Chou and the Shang had once ruled a united China; perhaps earlier emperors did too. But the new empire of Ch'in was larger and the iron-handed rule of the King of Ch'in was very different in character. The old title of king was no longer sufficient. The ruler of Ch'in reached back to the ancient golden age to choose a new title for himself. The Three August Ones were the San Huang and the Five Sovereigns the Su Ti. He combined the titles to Huang Ti, "August Sovereign," then added Shih to make his title "First August Sovereign." It was his intention that his son become the "Second August Sovereign," his grandson the "Third August Sovereign," and so on, for "Ten Thousand Generations." His dynasty did not survive long and he is often called "the Only First."

After attaining supreme power Ch'in Shih Huang Ti's acts seem to become more monstrous and irrational, and this is a good time to pause and consider the First Emperor's admirable qualities, for he did have them.

He united states which had been warring for centuries. How much of this success was due to Li Ssu, and how much to the First Emperor's own talents we will probably never know, but clearly the Only First had the ability to recognize administrative genius even if he did not possess it.

His reasons for conquest are sound enough: "If the whole world [and to the Chinese, China was the whole world] has suffered from unceasing warfare, this comes from there having been feudal lords and kings. Thanks to the aid of my ancestors, the empire has for the first time been pacified, and for me to restore feudal states would be to implant warfare. How difficult then to seek peace and repose."

The Emperor rejected Li Ssu's suggestion that he make members of his own family rulers of the newly created provinces. Instead, he chose men of ability without regard to rank or family. Each province had three administrators, one for the military, a second for the civil administration, and a third "directly responsible to the Emperor," whose job it was to spy on the other two.

Even the Emperor's worst enemies admitted that "usually he behaved decently to his men," but added "in the intoxication of success he only made them his victims."

In 221 B.C. Chin Shih Huang Ti was ruler of all China. He was the mightiest monarch in the world, and not just the world as China defined it. On the other side of the globe the Romans were locked in a death struggle with their enemy Hannibal, and the outcome was in doubt. The time of the Roman Empire was nearly two hundred years away. Even when Rome was at its height none of its emperors commanded the power of the Only First. In addition, the Lord of Ch'in established a basic administrative system that far outlasted the famed laws of the Romans.

After obliterating all the old states, the First Emperor tried to obliterate the past altogether by destroying all the works of history and literature. Li Ssu advised him that this was a wise course since it would eliminate, "dangerous thoughts" and prevent the use of "the past to discredit the present."

The only books exempted from this ban were those dealing with magic and practical books of instruction on subjects such as agriculture. The Emperor issued the order, hoping that from that day forward all history would begin with him.

If we think of the China of Ch'in Shih Huang Ti as a primitive nation, the full impact of this order cannot be appreciated. China was nothing of the sort; it was highly cultured, and already had a long and glorious history of which the Chinese were immensely proud. According to tradition 460 scholars went to their deaths defending their precious books. Some books were successfully hidden, others committed to memory, against the day when the tyrant would no longer sit on the throne. But, on the whole, the First Emperor's edict was tragically effective. Books of the time were laboriously written on bamboo strips, making them bulky and hard to conceal.

Says Ssu-ma Ch'ien, "Ch'in had unified the world." But how was the Emperor to hold it? The energies which until 221 B.C. had been concentrated on warfare were now turned toward the greatest building project of all times, the Great Wall of China.

To the north of China lay a vast grassy plain, unfit for agriculture, but fertile enough to support a thinly scattered population of stock-raising nomads. These nomads were divided into small, poverty-stricken and primitive tribes. But mounted on their sturdy little horses and armed with bows, which they used with deadly accuracy, the nomads made a mobile and highly effective fighting force. Life was unbelievably harsh for them and the lure of the rich farms and towns of China was irresistible. In periods when China was weak, or when the nomads organized, they were able to ride down and devastate the countryside.

There is a dispute as to whether or not the First Emperor built the Great Wall because he really feared nomadic attack. The nomads were not numerous, and almost always disorganized. A well-disciplined Chinese army could defeat them easily. Some experts believe that the Emperor ordered the construction of the Great Wall in order to absorb the energies of his own people.

In any event, the wall, in theory, would be an effective barrier. Not every section of so immense a rampart could be defended at all times. Nomads could launch a surprise attack at a weakly defended point, and could quickly scale the wall before the defenders could arrive. But while a man can climb a wall, a horse can't. Unmounted, the fighting efficiency of the nomads vanished. A more concentrated attack with battering rams could break a hole in the wall through which the horses could pass. But this took time and when such an attack was completed the invaders were likely to find a large Chinese army waiting for them on the other side.

The First Emperor entrusted the building of the Great Wall to one of his generals, Meng T'ien. Meng T'ien was able to incorporate many older walls, but still his accomplishment is awesome.

The Chinese developed no new engineering techniques in building the Great Wall; they merely applied their previous knowledge on a far vaster scale. The nature of the wall varied according to the local materials available, but in general it had these dimensions: It was 30 feet high, and 25 feet thick at the base, narrowing to about 15 feet at the top. Along the top there was a paved roadway that could be used by the army to move quickly from one section to another. On the northern side was a fortified zone of embankments, 200 yards wide.

About every 250 yards there were towers, averaging 35 feet

square and 45 feet high. Altogether, there were 25,000 of these towers. In addition, there were 15,000 detached towers, which served as extra watch towers and as beacon towers for signaling the approach of the enemy.

The Great Wall covers a distance of 1,400 miles, but if all the bends and kinks were straightened out the total length is 2,500 miles, the distance from New York City to Reno, Nevada.

In later times sections of the wall fell into ruin and were rebuilt, but by all accounts the original construction was excellent. It should have been, for the Only First decreed that any workman who left a crack between stones wide enough to put a nail in would be beheaded on the spot.

Construction went on summer and winter. The wall cut through burning deserts and snaked up torturous mountains. Tradition holds that a million men labored on the wall and that 400,000 died during the work. The accuracy of these figures is unknown, but the loss of life must have been awful. The Great Wall doubtless earned its title of "the longest cemetery in the world."

It took the Egyptians twenty years to complete the Great Pyramid. The Chinese built the much larger Great Wall in seven. Nor did the Great Wall quench Ch'in Shih Huang Ti's passion for building. He had a magnificent palace erected for himself—no, not a palace, a city of palaces, 270 of them, covering an area seventy miles in diameter. Unfortunately, the ruins of these palaces have never been excavated, and with only written records to rely upon, the descriptions of the royal compound sound unbelievable. Perhaps they are, but the Great Wall also sounds unbelievable.

Ch'in Shih Huang Ti spent the bulk of his final years roaming his enormous palace compound, secretly passing from one building to another by means of underground passages and never sleeping two nights in the same place. Perhaps he feared assassination, or he may have been acting in accordance with some obscure religious ritual. Or perhaps the First Emperor was losing his mind.

Section of the Great Wall

In 210 B.C., however, the Emperor did venture forth from his palaces. He was on an inspection trip of his empire when sickness overcame him, and he died more than a thousand miles from the capital.

The tomb in which the Only First was buried is also enveloped in legend. A great mound near the town of Lin T'ung, known as the "Mound of Ch'in," is believed to contain the remains of the tomb. Inside the tomb, the legends say, was an enormous bronze relief map of China. The Emperor's sarcophagus floated on rivers of quicksilver, modeled after the Yangtze and Yellow Rivers. If the tomb were violated, hidden springs fired stones and arrows at the intruders. A less attractive part of the picture was that those who built the tomb as well as many members of the royal household were buried alive inside.

What happened after the First Emperor's death is as sordid a tale of intrigue as the world has ever known. A sinister courtier named Chao Kao plotted with one of the Emperor's younger sons, Hu Hai, and the Grand Counselor Li Ssu to disinherit the rightful heir, Fu Su. Fu Su was tricked into committing suicide, and a little later Meng T'ien, builder of the Great Wall, was forced to accept the same fate.

Ancient carving of Chinese tiger

Next it was Li Ssu's turn. The wily Grand Counselor, who had survived so many years in the treacherous atmosphere of the court, seemed to have lost his touch. Chao Kao had Li Ssu and one of his sons implicated in a plot and executed. Chao Kao now exerted his evil influence on the weak emperor, finally succeeding in driving him mad, then inducing him to kill himself by telling him rebels had broken into the palace.

Chao Kao wanted to become emperor, but the court officials would not accept him and another son of Ch'in Shih Huang Ti was placed upon the throne. Shortly, a real revolt broke out. It had been simmering for a long time. Many groups combined to bring about the fall of the empire of Ch'in, but the man who finally reigned supreme was Liu Pang, a peasant who had started his rebellion with an army of ten ex-convicts. The young emperor was hunted down and executed, and the marvelous tomb of Ch'in Shih Huang Ti was ransacked. The First Emperor's palaces were set afire and, according to the stories, burned for three months.

So ended the time of the Ten Thousand Generations. Ch'in Shih Huang Ti's empire had lasted a little over a generation. Liu Pang, the peasant, founded the Han dynasty which endured 300 years. Yet Ch'in Shih Huang Ti cannot be ignored even today. His Great Wall was kept up for thousands of years. Most importantly, China never again returned to the mass of feudal states it had once been. His accomplishments, more than those of any other figure in Chinese history, enabled China, alone of all the ancient nations, to survive as an integrated culture. Even the name, China, comes from Ch'in.

Political conditions will probably keep archaeologists from filling in the record of this vital period for many years. But someday, when the palaces and tomb of Ch'in Shih Huang Ti are excavated, we can expect discoveries which equal or surpass those of any other nation in any period of history.

CHAPTER EIGHT

SUTTON HOO

The Empty Grave

FRESH FROM TRIUMPHS in Gaul, Julius Caesar came to Britain in 55 B.C. But Caesar was more interested in securing his military reputation than in risking it attempting to conquer this distant and wild land. Britain did not become part of the Roman empire until 43 A.D. when the Emperor Claudius traveled to the island to receive the surrender of the defeated Britons.

The British Isles are a long way from Rome and they always remained on the far fringes of the Empire. But for centuries Roman control held firm and the roots of Roman civilization sank deep into the land.

Yet when the Romans finally abandoned Britain in A.D. 425 there was little left to abandon. Roman rule throughout the world was collapsing under repeated barbarian invasions. Rather than fighting in distant lands, the hard-pressed Romans had been pulling their legions out of Britain to fight more important battles closer to home. To replace the legions the Romans invited in Germanic tribesmen. In return for military service, the barbarians were given extensive grants of land.

Thus, the barbarians, mainly from the tribes of Angles, Saxons, and Jutes, were already well entrenched when the Romans left.

These barbarians were continually reinforced by friends and relatives from their homelands who crossed the North Sea in great open rowing vessels. Known collectively as the Anglo-Saxons, they seized power from the Romans' failing hands. But they were a comparatively primitive people, who did not know what to do with what they had inherited. Towns, forts, and mansions were left unused. Once-fertile farms became flooded and useless as the Anglo-Saxons were unable to maintain the excellent Roman drainage systems. Communication became difficult as unrepaired roads crumbled into wreckage. The whole country slumped back into the conditions that had existed before the arrival of the Romans.

The Anglo-Saxons did not take to town life, and would not inhabit the decaying stone buildings they did not know how to repair. Nor did they need towns, for their simple economy did not demand centralization.

But even as ruins, the stone buildings, paved roads, and massive fortifications of the Romans were impressive. An early Anglo-Saxon work contains these lines: "Cities are visible from afar, the cunning work of giants, the wondrous fortifications in stone which are on this earth."

For almost four centuries England was plunged into darkness. Contemporary records are virtually non-existent and only a few obscure hints of the history of this period can be found in later documents. The bulk of what we know about early Anglo-Saxon life has come from archaeology.

The modern British are deeply interested in archaeology. Many of today's scientific techniques were developed in Britain, and many of the most significant archaeological discoveries throughout the world have been made by Englishmen. There is no other area in the world that has been as thoroughly and carefully explored archaeologically as the British Isles. Yet with all of this, solid evidence from the four centuries following the collapse of Roman Britain is still meager.

This is hardly surprising. By and large, the people of the time were wretchedly poor. They scratched a bare subsistence from the soil and were unable to collect the kind of material goods which delight and inform later archaeologists. A few huts of the sixth and early seventh century have been excavated. They are tiny squalid things, dug a few feet into the ground. The walls probably had been mud and the hut covered with thatch. The major surviving piece of early Anglo-Saxon literature, the epic *Beowulf*, speaks of grander habitations. Not castles, to be sure, but large timber halls for the aristocrats. None of these, however, has yet been found.

During this early period the inhabitants engaged in the unfortunate (from an archaeological point of view) practice of cremating their dead. The bodies were placed on a funeral pyre fully clothed and covered with their best ornaments. The burned remains were then placed in a bowl or jar and buried. Not much was left, so even when such a grave is found it yields little. Occasionally, though, the grave contains a hint as to the character of the man whose remains lie there. One grave had a collection of sheep bones, inscribed with magical symbols, and a set of bone playing-pieces, suggesting that their owner had been a confirmed gambler. But personal insights like this can rarely be gleaned from the graves of the early Anglo-Saxons.

Because of the poverty of most finds, the discovery of the great treasure ship at Sutton Hoo in 1939 is all the more remarkable. Sutton Hoo is in that part of England known in ancient times as East Anglia. It consists of the modern counties of Norfolk and Suffolk and lies on the eastern seaboard. It is only a short distance across the sea to the continent and the Anglo-Saxons were well established in the area early.

The Sutton Hoo burial ground itself is situated on the bank of the River Deben, opposite the town of Woodbridge, about ten miles from Ipswich. It was expected that something of archaeological interest would be found there. Some Anglo-Saxon burials are marked by mounds that archaeologists call barrows. There are a group of

The English Kingdoms
8th CENTURY A.D.

0   50   100
MILES

Northumbria

North

Sea

Irish   Sea

Lindsey

Wat's Dyke

Offa's Dyke

Welsh Kingdoms

Middle   Anglia

East
Anglia

SUTTON HOO

Essex

LONDON

Kent

Wessex   Sussex

Cornwall

English   Channel

sixteen barrows on a windy hill at Sutton Hoo, clearly visible from a
busy estuary which joins the sea six miles away. The largest mound
is oval-shaped and must have been at least 12 feet high and 100 feet
long when first constructed. Similar barrows had been opened be-

115

fore, but they had all been either plundered or humbly furnished. There was nothing from past experience which would have led the excavators to expect they would find a royal treasure ship.

Three or four hundred years ago grave robbers had attempted to plunder the barrow. The tunnel they dug was still visible. But the robbers lacked patience and became discouraged, abandoning their attempt just a few inches from the spot where objects of gold encrusted with precious stones lay.

A large open rowing ship, some 86 feet long and built for 36 oarsmen (a full 10 feet longer than the largest Viking ship ever found), had been dragged into a deep trench, filled with a royal treasure, and covered over with earth. Excavation of the Sutton Hoo ship burial was, in the words of W. F. Grimes, one of the archaeologists, an "exciting and exacting task."

The whole project was one of the greatest triumphs of the use of careful archaeological methods. The excavators were not simply digging up an old boat; in truth, none of the boat remained. Says the report on the excavation, "Since the whole ship and its contents had been involved in the sand for some 1,300 years, it is not surprising that there were virtually no remains of wood except for small fragments which were found here and there, preserving their form if not their character through contact with rusted iron. . . . Traces of the existence of wood could be frequently seen in the form of discoloured sand. . . ."

Carefully, inch by inch, the diggers proceeded—not with pick and shovel, but on their knees with broad-bladed knives and paint brushes. "None of the wood of the ship remained, though all the numerous clench-nails which had held its planking together were exactly in place; the ship had been completely filled up with as much of the sand excavated from the trench as could be got in again. These conditions were ideal for the preservation of its form. . . . By careful work from the inside it was possible to remove all the contents of the boat without displacing any of the nails, which remained

Interior of excavation at Sutton Hoo showing outline of burial ship

in their places on the sides of the excavations. This process was aided by a change in the consistency of the sand which was to be found where the boat's timbers once had been." Thus the excavation's report describes the tedious process.

After 1,300 years, not a boat, but the ghost of a long-vanished boat emerged from the sand of East Anglia, its timbers reduced to a layer of discolored sand. The interior of this phantom boat contained the richest Anglo-Saxon find ever made and, according to some, the most splendid archaeological discovery ever made in the British Isles.

In the center of the ship the burial party had erected a wooden cabin, and in it they deposited the personal effects of the chieftain in whose honor they had dragged the ship up from the estuary and buried it in the sandy heath.

The treasure of the Sutton Hoo ship burial today is on display

117

in the British Museum. Among the objects found were forty-one of solid gold, encrusted with garnets. Everywhere there was evidence of the warlike nature of the owner: a six-foot iron standard topped with the emblem of a stag, a gold-handled sword, a great shield, and a coat of mail. The crushed remains of the warrior king's helmet were there; it must have been an impressive piece of armor, ornamented with bronze and silver plaques and provided with pieces to protect the wearer's ears and neck. On the front of the helmet was a hinged visor to protect his face. The visor was made in the form of a fearsome mask worked in bronze, silver, and garnet. Yet the importance of the Sutton Hoo find—in fact, of any archaeological find— is not the monetary value of the objects, but what they tell us about the people who made and used them. Sutton Hoo provides a point of light in an obscure and confused but extremely important period in the history of the development of English society and therefore in the development of our own society.

The burial had all the form and accoutrements of a royal grave. Who was the royal personage buried there? The answer to this question gave the archaeologists their biggest surprise, for the barrow contained no body at all, and it probably never had. "The absence of human remains did not of itself provoke comment," wrote C. W. Phillips, one of the archaeologists on the scene, "because the conditions of this grave set deep in damp sand were most unfavorable to the survival of any organic remains."

Although most of the people of East Anglia cremated their dead, the rulers customarily were buried. But as the objects were removed, the excavators found that "there was really no room for the proper laying out of a body at the more honourable end of the grave, nor were there any of those smaller, more personal objects found which would have been on a clothed body."

The puzzled archaeologists made elaborate chemical tests of the entire length of the ship. They found not a trace of human remains. The burial must have been what archaeologists call a ceno-

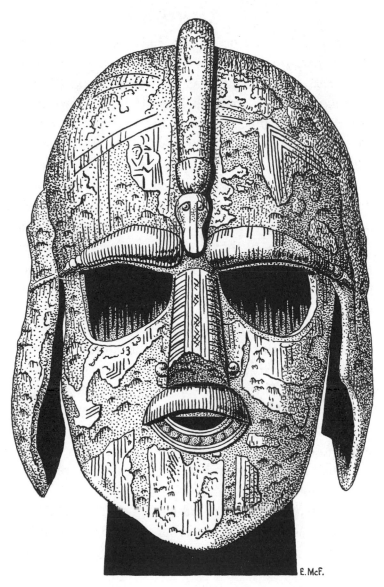

Helmet visor in form of warrior's face found at Sutton Hoo

taph, an empty tomb meant for a person whose body had been
destroyed or was buried elsewhere. Monuments of this type are not
uncommon in history. But who was it meant for? Scholars began to
put the pieces of the puzzle together.

Clearly, the Sutton Hoo ship burial was meant for a man of high rank, probably a king or another member of the royal house. A great scepter, symbol of royal power, was one of the objects found. "It was projecting upwards," says Phillips, who witnessed the excavation, "and the sinister-looking bearded human heads carved on the emergent end gave it a daunting look."

Starting around the year 500, groups of northern Anglo-Saxons from Scandinavia began migrating to East Anglia and soon dominated the area. Archaeologists call these invaders the Ipswich People, from a large cemetery found at that place. Documents tell us that the royal family of this new wave of invaders was called the Wuffings, after Wuffa, one of the early kings of the dynasty. His father was leader of the Ipswich People when they migrated to England. Originally the Wuffings had come from an area in Sweden where ship-burial had been practiced. It is the only other place in the world where this distinctive form of burial is known from that era, and it is reasonable to assume that the immigrants brought the tradition with them. The sword, shield, and helmet were of Scandinavian design, probably carried to England and passed on as family heirlooms. There were great drinking horns, with silver mounts, some large enough to hold six quarts of liquid. These are objects we identify exclusively with the Vikings, yet here they were among the effects of an English king.

Height of Wuffing power in East Anglia was reached about 610 under the rule of Raedwald. But his successors were unable to resist the growing strength of larger neighboring kingdoms. After Raedwald's death, four other Wuffing kings fell in battle, unsuccessfully trying to defend their kingdom. East Anglia was destined to become a satellite kingdom to its more powerful neighbors, and its monarchs were reduced to the status of puppets.

Dating the time of the burial at Sutton Hoo was made relatively easy when excavators unearthed a purse containing thirty-seven gold coins struck in the kingdom of the Merovingian Franks in France.

Coins of this type were made around 650. The presence of a heavy bronze bowl made in Alexandria, Egypt, bowls from Ireland, and silver dishes made in the Byzantine Empire testify that the Anglo-Saxon aristocracy used their sea power to import luxury goods from many parts of the world.

There were humbler objects too, but these were in a perilous state. The excavation report notes: "A hot drying sun poured into the bottom of the ship. If they were to be preserved for future treatment it was obvious that the best hope for their preservation would lie in a reconstruction of the conditions which had already preserved them for many hundreds of years. Cups, gourds and the like were packed in damp moss and cotton while pillows, shoes, and other fabrics or leather objects were put in bowls of water." Every stage of the excavation was carefully photographed lest any detail be lost.

The ship burial gave tantalizing hints about the confused religious picture in East Anglia during the Dark Ages. The Roman Britons had been thoroughly Christianized. The invading Anglo-Saxons, however, brought with them the pagan beliefs of their forefathers, and were not quick to give up their ancient religion and adopt that of the conquered people. The spread of Christianity among the Anglo-Saxons was slow and spotty. Raedwald was converted in about 617, according to a Church account of the Christianization of England, one of the few surviving written documents of this period. But Raedwald's conversion was less than complete, for the Church account notes that on the advice of his pagan wife "and certain false teachers" Raedwald retained altars "for offerings made to the devils." The devils were the old gods of the Anglo-Saxons. For a time the East Anglian kingship passed back and forth between Christian and pagan monarchs.

The buried ship contained two silver spoons inscribed "Saulos" and "Paulos," the names of Saul and Paul in Greek. The spoons had been made in the Byzantine Empire and were undoubtedly Christian artifacts, probably baptismal presents for a Christian convert. Other objects seem also to have come from the household of a king who was at least a nominal Christian. Church records attest that East Anglia was almost completely Christian by 650. But despite all of this, Sutton Hoo does not really look like a Christian burial. "The whole taken together is still the provision for the passage to Valhalla," says Phillips.

Here, then, is a possible reason for the empty grave. If the king were a Christian his body would have to be buried in consecrated ground adjacent to newly-founded monasteries and churches. But in a place where Christianity represented only a thin, and recently acquired, covering for an essentially pagan society an additional old-style monument may have been constructed as sort of an insurance policy, in case Christianity did not provide sufficient protection in the afterlife. Phillips theorizes that the king "was in fact a Christian and was buried elsewhere in consecrated ground, though family custom and public policy still required this expensive and essentially pagan monument to his memory."

An alternate explanation advanced for the empty grave is that it was constructed for a man whose body was lost at sea, or lost in battle.

Purse lid from Sutton Hoo

A popular candidate for ownership of the Sutton Hoo ship is King Anna, who died in battle in 654. But Anna was, according to records, a devout Christian who gave his life trying to repel a pagan invasion of East Anglia. Four of his daughters are known to have entered religious communities. This does not entirely fit with the basically pagan nature of the burial. Another candidate is Anna's brother Aethelhere, a pagan or lapsed Christian who was killed in a flood during a battle in 655. David M. Wilson of the British Museum favors Aethelhere. "My own view is that the Sutton Hoo cenotaph commemorates Aethelhere, the pagan king, whose body was not available to his followers when they erected his grave. In this heroic age one of the greatest things a man could do was to die on the field of battle. Aethelhere, despite his short reign, died the death of a hero and would therefore be deemed worthy by his followers of receiving the burial due to a pagan hero." King Ecgric who died in the early 640's has also been mentioned, but, in truth, the name of the owner of the ship at Sutton Hoo remains unknown.

Perhaps further research will provide it. Shortly after the opening of the ship burial in 1939 virtually all archaeological activity in Britain was suspended by the beginning of World War II. At the time only four of the sixteen barrows had been opened. These were hastily recovered and the area was converted into a battle school. Some of the barrows were damaged when tanks were driven over them during the war, and for over a quarter of a century excavations at the site were limited. In 1967 the British Museum announced that full-scale excavations at Sutton Hoo would begin again. The present plans call for the opening of a new mound each year for the next twelve years. The archaeologists are also planning to construct a full-scale wooden replica of the original ship.

The ship itself had been the most important part of the burial. The ships had brought the Anglo-Saxons across the sea to their new home, and with the ships they were able to maintain contact with the more advanced parts of the world. Clearly, the Anglo-Saxons recognized the importance of the ship to their society. Sutton Hoo is not the only ship burial in the British Isles, although it is by far the largest and most impressive. At Snape, another unknown chieftain who died around 635 was placed beneath a barrow in a 50-foot ship. Sadly, this burial was looted in ancient times. At another spot archaeologists discovered about a dozen graves from the same era, which had not been filled with earth but covered with timbers from a ship's side. Archaeologists view these "pseudo ship-burials" as poor men's versions of Sutton Hoo.

The principal meaning of the find at Sutton Hoo is that the Dark Ages of the early Anglo-Saxon period are not as dark as we had believed. Wilson sums it up thus: "The unknown king has left his memorial and we can only admire the riches and glories of these East Anglian kings who numbered among their treasures the finest jewelry produced in Europe at that time, as well as riches imported from the exotic Mediterranean world. The king who was commemorated by this burial must be seen as the peer of any Germanic or Saxon king in Western Europe."

CHAPTER NINE

QUETZALCOATL

Bringer of Civilization

GOD OR MAN, Quetzalcoatl, the plumed serpent, is the most enigmatic figure in the history of America before the coming of Columbus, and one of the most important.

The name and image of Quetzalcoatl can be found in many places throughout Middle America. He was worshipped by many of the ancient peoples, most notably the Toltecs and Mayans. But thirty years ago most archaeologists regarded Quetzalcoatl as nothing more than a legend. Yet written records gave a clear, if rather exaggerated, account of the life of a real historical king named Quetzalcoatl, whose life had been incorporated into the legends of the god with the same name.

Fernando de Alva Ixtilxochitl, a descendant of the old kings of Mexico, wrote extensively of Quetzalcoatl in the history of his people which he compiled in the sixteenth century. The Franciscan friar, Father Bernardino de Sahagún, one of the few among the early Spanish who made a real attempt to understand the conquered Indians, also collected and recorded the tales of Quetzalcoatl.

The stories vary in detail, but according to all of them, Quetzalcoatl was a god who came to earth as a chief of the Toltecs and ruled a great empire during an ancient golden age. The seat of Quet-

125

zalcoatl's empire was the city of Tula.

Mexican archaeology started comparatively late. During the early years of this century Toltec remains were almost unknown, and the site of ancient Tula had been lost or, more accurately, it was being ignored. In 1940 Mexican archaeologists began studying the ruins near a modern village called Tula, and they began turning legend into history. Here, near its contemporary namesake, was ancient Tula, capital of the Toltec empire and home of the fabled Quetzalcoatl. The Indians had known this all along, but no one believed them.

Today Mexican archaeology is booming. An enormous mass of information has been accumulated about the pre-Columbian Americans. The picture is not a simple one, and there are still many mysterious gaps, but the outlines are beginning to emerge. Central America contained a host of different cultures—Maya, Aztec, Toltec, and others—but they are all related, racially and culturally. In a strange way the story of the rise and sudden fall of pre-Columbian civilizations is paralleled in the haunting legend of the rise and fall of Quetzalcoatl.

When the Toltec civilization was first being discovered archaeologists thought they had found the "mother culture" for all the groups that followed. Now we know that the Toltecs were latecomers who borrowed much from earlier peoples. The first civilized people of Mexico had been entirely forgotten. Only modern archaeology has been able to rescue them from oblivion.

Mexican civilization began with a little-known people—the Olmecs. The Aztecs called the tribes that lived in the swamps and hills of the southern part of the Gulf coast of Mexico the Olmeca Huixtotin, "the Rubber People of the South." But two thousand years before the Aztecs appeared a high civilization flourished in this area. We call them the Olmecs, although we do not know what they called themselves.

Only now are Olmec artifacts being unearthed in any great numbers. There has never been anything quite like Olmec art. Most famous are the enormous round, stone heads, with their flat, thick-featured, strangely baby-like faces. Even weirder are the numerous chubby little clay figures. Dr. Michael Coe of Yale University, probably the world's leading expert on the Olmecs, sees in the grotesque but immature features of these figures a reflection of the face of the largest of American wild cats, the jaguar.

Olmec civilization began, as far as we know, around 900 B.C. Its influence was widespread throughout Mexico, but around 400 B.C. the Olmecs seem to have abandoned their towns. Thousands of monuments were broken, or if this was too difficult, mutilated and carefully buried.

Surely there must have been an overpowering reason for this time-consuming, systematic destruction. Dr. Coe postulates a revolution of some sort. But who were the rebels and what were they fighting for or against? We simply do not know.

About a century before the Olmecs disappeared a people we call the Zapotecs began building their imposing mountaintop sanctuary of Monte Alban. Of all the pre-Columbian groups the Zapotecs seem the most stable, surviving intact for almost two thousand years until they fell to the Aztecs at the end of the twelfth century.

Next came the most famous of all pre-Columbian civilization—the Mayan. Archaeologists have dated the first of the Maya stone buildings at about 300 B.C. The Maya have the most complex history of all the peoples of pre-Columbian America. The term Mayan describes a large group of tribes speaking similar languages and having a similar culture. But the Mayans lacked political or national unity. Independent cities rose and fell throughout the Maya area over a long period, leaving the archaeologists with a tangled history to try to sort out. But again we see the phenomenon of great cities destroyed and abandoned for no apparent reason.

In the two centuries before the birth of Christ a people (we don't have any name at all for them) built a really enormous city near present-day Mexico City. The temples of this city took the shape of pyramids and the largest, which is called the Pyramid of

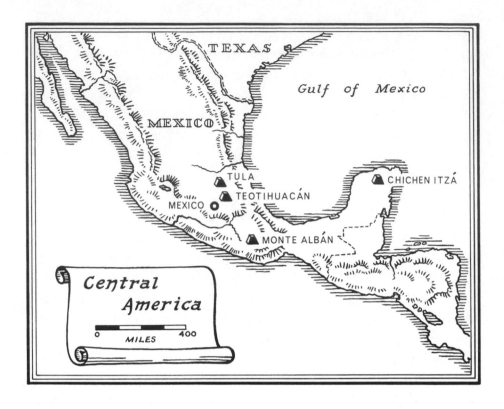

the Sun is, in some of its dimensions, even larger than the Great Pyramid of Khufu in Egypt. The city was in ruins when the Aztecs came to Mexico. It had lasted six centuries and had fallen suddenly, violently, and mysteriously. But the ruins were still impressive and the Aztecs called the place Teotihuacan, "the place where gods were made."

At the time Teotihuacan fell the whole of Mexico seemed to be undergoing a vast convulsion which destroyed all the old centers of power. Into the vacuum left by this upheaval came the Toltecs. But from where did they come? At first, archaeologists thought they must have come from the north, from parts of what is now the United States. Now opinion has swung toward a southern origin. They must have moved into Mexico during the sixth century; at least that is the date given to the earliest Toltec artifacts. By 750 A.D. they were living in Tula.

128

The Toltecs, according to some of the Indian histories, were led by a chief called Mixcoatl, who forged an empire. Mixcoatl was assassinated by one of his captains who usurped the throne. Before his death Mixcoatl had married a woman who was a native of Mexico. When he was killed, his pregnant wife, Chimalman, escaped and hid with her parents. Chimalman died while giving birth to Mixcoatl's son.

The child was called Ce Acatl Topiltzin, but he later took the name Quetzalcoatl. The *quetzal* is a beautifully feathered bird which is still found in the jungles of Central America and *coatl* means snake—hence, his symbol of the feathered serpent.

The story of the child reared in exile has given rise to this theory: Quetzalcoatl was an ancient god of the people of Mexico, but was not worshipped by the invading Toltecs. King Mixcoatl married a woman from the conquered people, and when his son was raised by his mother's family he adopted their worship of Quetzalcoatl, whose name he later took. Since Mexican kings were religious as well as political leaders, it was a common practice for them to take a god's name. An added confusion results because other priests also took this name and this has led to attributing the acts of the god, the king, and the numerous priests all to a single semi-divine individual.

While he was still young, Quetzalcoatl led a rebellion among the Toltecs, and killed the usurper in battle. Quetzalcoatl was now undisputed king of the Toltecs and, say the legends, he initiated a golden age. His most important contribution was teaching his people to sow corn, "the perfect crop" in the opinion of the Indians. He also instructed them in the arts of writing and architecture and gave them the calendar. Among the many civilizing influences the king exercised upon his people was that he barred the practice of human sacrifice, a brutal ritual and part of the dark side of the religion of pre-Columbian Mexico.

Here, according to one theory is what actually happened: The new king had inherited much of the wisdom of the older high civilizations of Mexico and through his influence this advanced culture was passed on to the Toltecs who had come to Mexico as barbarous invaders.

All good things were attributed to the person of King Quetzalcoatl. We know, however, that corn was being grown in Mexico a long time before the Toltec invasion. The calendar was being used by the Maya (and probably by the Olmecs) hundreds of years earlier. The building of all Tula was ascribed to Quetzalcoatl, although archaeologists have shown conclusively that the city had been built over a long period, extending both before and after the time of King Quetzalcoatl. The process by which the Toltecs assimilated Mexican culture must have taken generations.

In the legends the downfall of Quetzalcoatl was brought about through the machinations of evil gods and wizards led by the crafty Tezcatlipoca. Here, too, scholars now believe that the legend describes a real historical event, most probably a struggle between two Toltec groups. The first was either led by King Quetzalcoatl or by the priests who worshipped the god of that name; the second was probably a military group owing its allegiance to the fierce old god, Tezcatlipoca. The conflict probably led to a disastrous civil war shortly after 980, in which Tula was burned and at least for a time abandoned.

Father Bernardino de Sahagún's story of the fall of Quetzalcoatl says: "Many other evil things befell the Toltecs and brought about the ending of their good fortune. Quetzalcoatl, troubled and saddened . . . was determined that he must go, and abandon his beautiful city. He had everything burned; his houses of silver and coral, the House of Gold, and all the treasures of art. The treasures of costly things he buried, hiding them in the mountains and ravines beside the rivers . . . When all was done he took his road and departed from Tula."

The legends go on to relate how Quetzalcoatl and a few of his

Quetzalcoatl

followers wandered throughout Mexico, finally reaching the coast and setting sail to the east. But before he left, Quetzalcoatl vowed that someday he would return again from the east. This promise was to have fateful consequences for Mexico.

Some of the legends say that the Toltecs under Quetzalcoatl sailed to Yucatan and established themselves there in the area of the city of Chichen Itzá. Yucatan was a stronghold of the Maya peoples, but archaeological exploration of the site of Chichen Itzá shows clear Toltec influences.

Here the story of Quetzalcoatl cannot be clearly related to historical events. We know there was a Toltec invasion of Yucatan but it took place long after the fall of the Toltec empire, and could not possibly have been led by the same famous King Quetzalcoatl. Nor were the Toltec invaders of Yucatan anything like the followers of the king who preached an end to human sacrifice. Like most of the Central American Indians, the Maya practiced human sacrifice, but it was infrequent in every part of the Maya domain except for Chichen Itzá, once it fell under the influence of the Toltec invaders.

The Spanish told horror-filled tales of the rites at the sacrificial well at Chichen Itzá. Many believed the stories to be mere propaganda aimed at establishing the moral superiority of the Spanish over the savage natives. In recent years archaeologists equipped with diving gear have descended into the deep forbidding waters of the sacred well. There they found human remains that could not possibly have been the result of accidental drowning. Not as many skele-

Toltec temple

Maya representation of Quetzalcoatl

tons as might have been expected from the Spanish accounts were found—but there were enough to show that the stories were not a complete fabrication.

The problem of the Toltec penetration of Yucatan is a sticky one for the scholars. Clearly, the conquest of Chichen Itzá by Quetzalcoatl is a legendary simplification of a later Toltec invasion of that area. But what had the Toltecs been doing in the long dark period between the fall of their Mexican empire and their appearance in Yucatan? In addition, there is a startling similarity between Chichen Itzá and the old Toltec capital of Tula. "It seems almost as if the same architects had supervised the construction of both cities, only in Chichen they added Mayan ideas which they found on the spot," says Ignacio Bernal, Director of the National Museum of Anthropology in Mexico.

If the Toltecs of Yucatan were not led by Quetzalcoatl the king, they certainly remembered Quetzalcoatl the god, except that there his name was translated into the Mayan language as Kulkulcan, which also means plumed serpent.

The Maya hated their Toltec masters and regarded them as inferiors. The one surviving Mayan document from the area, the so-called *Book of the Jaguar Priest*, scornfully refers to the Toltecs as "those who speak poorly." The book deplores the loose morals and barbarous ways of the newcomers. Ultimately the Maya of Chichen Itzá either rose up and overthrew the Toltec overlords or

133

absorbed them. Toltec influence disappeared and only much later were archaeologists able to determine that the Toltecs had ever been there.

Obviously the legend of Quetzalcoatl played an important part in the history and development of the Indian civilizations of Central America, but it was to play its most important role centuries after the death of the ruler who had done so much to inspire it. Indeed, if Quetzalcoatl was credited with the beginning of Mexican civilization he can also be, in a sense, blamed for its disastrous fall.

There were some very odd features about Quetzalcoatl. Father Sahagún offers this description of the pyramid at Tula: "At the top of the pyramid stood the statue of Quetzalcoatl, covered with mantles. It was terrifyingly ugly, and had a huge battered stone for its head which had a very long and hideous beard." The image of a bearded Quetzalcoatl appears again and again throughout Mexico, in both Toltec and Mayan art. (It must be noted, however, that Quetzalcoatl was not always depicted as a bearded man.) Then, too, the legends speak of Quetzalcoatl as wearing a white robe, or in some cases of actually having a white skin.

When Quetzalcoatl sailed off into the Gulf of Mexico he made this promise to his people. "On the date of my birth which is Ce-Acatl, the year of 1-Reed—I will return." The date was of enormous importance. The Indians of Mexico, who had developed such an excellent calendar, ultimately became enslaved by their own invention. They were obsessed with time and the date upon which an event occurred had a significance far beyond that which it is given in European culture. Unlike the Western calendar, the Indian calendar does not progress ever forward, but depicts human events as occurring in cycles. Thus, according to Mexican calculations the date of Quetzalcoatl's birth, the year 1-Reed, could fall, for example, in the years 1363, 1467, and 1519.

By what must surely be one of the most astounding coincidences in history, the Spanish conqueror Hernando Cortez and his party landed in Mexico in 1519—Ce-Acatl, the year of 1-Reed, and the year of the promised return of Quetzalcoatl. These bearded white men fitted perfectly the legendary descriptions of Quetzalcoatl. One of the first gifts sent to Cortez by Montezuma, emperor of the Aztecs, was a magnificent headdress of quetzal plumes—the symbol of the departed god.

Rumors of the return of Quetzalcoatl had circulated among the Aztecs for a long time. Columbus had made contact with the Maya in his fourth and last voyage in 1502, and from that time until Cortez' small fleet landed at Vera Cruz, stories of the mysterious comings and goings of bearded white men were told and retold, doubtless magnified in each retelling as they were passed from the coast to the heartland of the Aztecs. By the time Cortez set foot in Mexico the entire Aztec empire was in a state of profound insecurity and depression because of the rumors of Quetzalcoatl's return.

Cortez was not confronting a primitive people, or even a weak and decadent empire. The Aztecs were warriors of terrifying skill and ferocity. Not long before the coming of the Spanish they had conquered the entire valley of Mexico. Yet they crumbled before a relative handful of Spanish soldiers. They would have fallen eventually anyway, for there is no chance that the Indians of Mexico could have forever withstood the advanced military techniques and weapons of Europe. But the legend of Quetzalcoatl must have contributed to the speed of their decline.

Still, to many the destruction of the Aztecs seems freakishly abrupt. It isn't really. In many parts of Mexico the Indians fought long and valiantly before being overwhelmed by superior forces. Then, too, for all the splendor of the great Indian civilizations there was a basic instability about them. As we have seen, they rose and fell regularly, long before the coming of the Spaniards. It seems that civil war played a large part in the destruction of previous cultures; the legend of the fall of Quetzalcoatl clearly indicates this. Cortez skillfully played upon the resentments of the Aztecs' subjects.

Despite their impressive façade of power, the rulers of the Indian states must have lived in constant fear of overthrow by their miserably oppressed subjects. Perhaps the regularity with which empires fell gave the Indians their pessimistic idea of time as a series of repeating cycles. Perhaps, too, that is why all Mexico had waited so hopefully and fearfully for the return of Quetzalcoatl, who would bring back the morality and justice of the golden age to the land. Any hopes they might have had were to be bitterly disappointed. Cortez was no Quetzalcoatl, no matter how he may have resembled the god physically.

The description of Quetzalcoatl as a bearded white man presents a fascinating problem. The Indians of Mexico are not white and rarely bearded. Quetzalcoatl is spoken of as the god who brought many of the advances of civilization to the people of Central America. Is it possible that at some point early in the history of the development of pre-Columbian civilization in Central America a bearded white man, or a group of bearded white men, somehow reached the New World, and imparted to the still primitive Indians knowledge from the more advanced civilizations of Europe? The theory has been seriously advanced many times. Everyone from the Phoenicians to the Vikings have been proposed for the honor. Even early Christian missionaries have been seen as the real inspiration for the Quetzalcoatl legends. Supporters of this theory cite Quetzalcoatl's abhorrence of human sacrifice, and note that some of the legends state that during his wanderings Quetzalcoatl marked places where he had been by shooting an arrow into a tree. This, the theory runs, resembles a cross.

The idea of European "culture bearers" is attractive and flattering to people of European origin, but most archaeologists reject it today. No European artifacts, dating from before the Spanish conquest have ever been found in Mexico. Quetzalcoatl's great accomplishment was supposed to have been bringing the cultivation of corn to the Indians, yet the Europeans did not grow corn—they

Façade from temple of Quetzalcoatl, the plumed serpent

learned about it from the Indians. The Indians also possessed a better calendar and their system of writing is totally different from any found in Europe.

The stories concerning Quetzalcoatl's white skin are questionable. They were all collected by the Spanish. The Spanish were eager to legitimize their conquest, and may have interpreted Quetzalcoatl's white robe as a white skin. Or they simply may have misunderstood what the Indians told them. On the other hand, the Indians must have been eager to please their new masters by telling them what they wanted to hear.

The beards are another matter. Quetzalcoatl's beard is obvious on many pieces of sculpture carved long before the coming of the Spanish. Although beards are rare among the Indians, Quetzalcoatl is not the only bearded figure known in pre-Columbian America.

137

Men with beards are shown on statues dating all the way back to the time of the Olmecs. In 1967 archaeologists announced the discovery of Olmec paintings in a Mexican cave. They are the oldest paintings ever found in the New World. One of them shows a bearded man. It is possible that the unusual Indian who was able to grow a beard was considered to have some sort of special power. Unusual physical features are often worshipped. The Olmecs, it seems, worshipped deformed children. If the beard were regarded as a special mark, it is not illogical to assume that the Indians would have depicted their primary god as a man possessing this special mark. Perhaps the Toltec king known as Quetzalcoatl really did have a beard.

There is another possibility. In Japan there exists a small group of people known as the Ainu. They are white-skinned and heavily bearded. The Ainu live among the yellow-skinned, beardless Japanese. No one knows where they came from, but they are a very ancient people who lived in Japan before the Mongolian Japanese arrived. Ainu legends say that they came from the sky and they speak of themselves as the Sky People. Could a similar group have existed among the Indians of South America and given them the idea later embodied into the tales of bearded, white-skinned Quetzalcoatl? There is no solid evidence to support this theory, yet the idea is every bit as plausible as the theory of "culture bearers" from Europe.

The story of Quetzalcoatl, the strange, kindly, bearded god-man who walked through Mexico long before the coming of the Europeans, remains unfinished. Part of the tale we know is true, for we have found the city of Tula, which a king called Quetzalcoatl once ruled. As for the rest, we simply don't know. In tracing this legend archaeologists of the Americas may yet uncover some truly startling finds.

CHAPTER TEN

LEIF ERICSSON

Voyager to Vinland

THE VIKINGS who lived in Greenland and Iceland had their own tales about the discovery of America, except that they didn't call it America.

In the year 986 a young man named Bjarne Herjulfsson sailed to Iceland to find his father Herjulf. (The Norse added their father's name; thus, Herjulfsson means exactly what it sounds like—Herjulf's son.) Bjarne was told that his father had joined a party which had migrated to Greenland, a land recently discovered by Eric the Red. The new land, it was said, was not too far, so Bjarne decided to seek his father there.

He received exact instructions as to where to sail, but his ship ran into a fog and he got lost. For days Bjarne's ship wandered aimlessly until finally land was sighted. Bjarne was puzzled by what he saw, for the Icelanders had told him that Greenland had high mountains, and the land in front of him had no mountains, only barren low hills. So he sailed on. He sighted land two more times, but neither of these places fitted the description of Eric's Greenland, and Bjarne did not bother to go ashore. Finally his sails caught a northeast wind and after a passage through the open sea he sighted land for the fourth time. At last he had found a place that looked like Greenland, and as he stepped ashore he was greeted by his father.

139

Bjarne naturally told about the land to the west he had found, and other Greenland Vikings became interested in exploring it. Most interested of all was Eric the Red's son, Leif Ericsson.

Leif bought Bjarne's ship and with thirty-five men set off, following Bjarne's instructions. Using the prevailing ocean currents, Leif was easily able to reach the first of the landfalls Bjarne had mentioned. But it was an unpromising place of rocks rubbed smooth by ancient glaciers. Leif called it Helluland or the "Land of Flat Stones." Nothing there attracted the Vikings. Sailing southward, he reached a wooded area which he named Markland or Woodland. Still, it did not look like a good place to land and the voyage continued south. Then Leif and his men came upon "Vinland the Good."

Here the stories became ecstatic about how rich and wonderful this land was. Vinland was covered with grapes, from which wine could be made (and for centuries everyone assumed that Vinland meant "Wineland" or land of grape vines). The grass was magnificent for cattle and was so rich that, according to one tale, butter dripped from the end of every blade.

Leif returned with his wonderful account, and more Vikings prepared to sail to the western paradise. Leif's brother Thorvald, again using Bjarne's ship, set out in 1004, but upon landing encountered trouble, and the image of paradise was shattered.

When the Vikings came to Iceland and Greenland they found uninhabited islands, but Vinland had a native population and the natives were suspicious and not at all friendly. Thorvald's party was attacked by "ugly little men" and Thorvald himself was killed.

Still, the Vikings were not discouraged. More expeditions set out. Colonies were established and flourished, possibly for hundreds of years. Then, for a variety of reasons, the Viking expansion ended and darkness fell over Vinland and ultimately over Greenland as well. This promising start ended in barrenness and was all but forgotten.

Viking ship

We know where Greenland is. That giant ice-covered island retains its Viking name to this day. But where is Vinland? If the legends are to be believed, Vinland could only be the east coast of North America. This means that Bjarne and Leif discovered America five centuries before Christopher Columbus' historic voyage in 1492. But were the Greenland and Iceland sagas to be believed?

For a very long time no one bothered about the Norse legends. The Scandinavian countries, home of the Vikings, became isolated from the mainstream of Western civilization. It was not until 1705 that a Danish scholar, Thormant Torfaeus, proposed the idea that the legendary Vinland was the real North America. Over the years this theory attracted a considerable following, but it was never entirely accepted. So many of the Viking legends were filled with mythical events that it was hard to believe anything in them without confirming evidence. The sort of evidence necessary would be the discovery of Viking ruins somewhere in North America.

Viking artifacts of sorts were found all over the coast and as far inland as Minnesota, but these were either of questionable authenticity, or downright fraudulent. So, until a few years ago, the question remained unsettled.

A problem for those looking for Vinland was that they assumed the word meant "Wineland" or a place where grapes grew in abundance. If this were true it meant that Leif must have landed to the south of the present location of New York City; grapes do not grow well north of that point. The search ranged as far south as the Virginia coast. Locating the spot on the seemingly endless coastline began to look hopeless, particularly since it was doubtful that Viking ruins would be either large or obvious.

A Norwegian explorer and archaeologist, Dr. Helge Ingstad, had spent years searching the coast for evidence of the Vikings in America, but in vain. Finally he decided to change his approach to the problem. First, with an expert on languages, he attacked the word "vin" from Vinland. Did it really mean wine or vines? Wine would have been very pleasant for Leif and his men, but not necessary. Another possible meaning for the old Norse word "vin" is grass or pasturage; thus, Vinland may have meant "grassland" or "pasture land." If Leif was looking for a place to start a settlement, a spot that had good grazing land for cattle would have been far more attractive than a place with grapes for wine. Dr. Ingstad reasoned that Vinland might have been far to the north of the grape-growing region, and much closer to Greenland from whence Leif's voyage commenced.

Dr. Ingstad, himself an experienced sailor, then tried to put himself in Leif Ericsson's position. How would the Viking have planned the trip? "He could sit in his hall in Brattahlid in Greenland," said Dr. Ingstad, "and in the concise way of speech that is reflected in the sagas, tell one of the sea captains what landmarks and on what schedule he would reach Vinland." Studying the sagas carefully, Dr. Ingstad decided that Leif would first have followed the warm current north along the coast of Greenland, then sail out

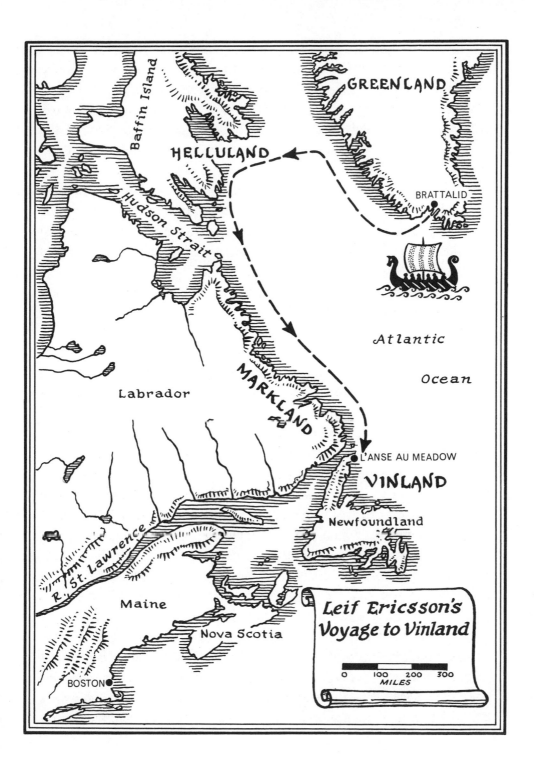

GREENLAND

Baffin Island

HELLULAND

BRATTALID

Hudson Strait

Atlantic

Ocean

MARKLAND

Labrador

L'ANSE AU MEADOW

VINLAND

Newfoundland

R. St. Lawrence

Maine

Nova Scotia

BOSTON

Leif Ericsson's Voyage to Vinland

0   100   200   300
MILES

of sight of land across the Davis Strait until he saw the rocky coast of Helluland, present-day Baffin Island, then along the wooded shore of Markland, which Dr. Ingstad identified with Labrador. By carefully examining the wording of the sagas Dr. Ingstad arrived at the conclusion that "Grassland" must be on Newfoundland. "You can't miss it," he said.

It wasn't all that easy. During the 1950's Dr. Ingstad traveled through Newfoundland looking for landmarks mentioned in the sagas, and asking questions. Then one day a fisherman told him that he had heard of some ruins near the little village of L'Anse au Meadow, on the northern tip of the island.

It was not surprising that no one had heard of the ruins before. The village contains only eleven families. No highways lead to it. L'Anse au Meadow is so isolated that its residents still speak an antiquated English dialect. (They call their village Lancy Meadows.) A local fisherman named George Decker led Dr. Ingstad to the ruins and told him, "No stranger has seen them, and here at Lancy Meadows nobody tramps around without me knowing it."

There was not much to see, just the barely visible traces of ancient walls. But they looked promising enough for Dr. Ingstad to form an expedition and begin excavations the following year. The outlines of the settlement which gradually emerged from the earth were quite recognizable to experts on the Vikings. The "great hall" of the settlement, which measured 70 by 55 feet, was strikingly similar to the hall of Brattahlid in Greenland where Leif had lived. So close was the resemblance that Dr. Ingstad speculated that not only had he found a Viking settlement (for there must have been many) but that this was the *Leifsbodarna* (Leif's land) itself.

Around the hall the remains of six other houses were found. In addition, Dr. Ingstad's wife, Anne Stine Ingstad, an archaeologist in her own right, excavated a Viking smithy where the settlers had practiced a primitive form of iron processing in much the same way as the Vikings of Scandinavia did. Charcoal from the site was dated by the Carbon-14 method. The dates centered around the year 1000, the time of Leif's voyage.

No spectacular artifacts were found at L'Anse au Meadow. It was not a large settlement and probably had not been occupied for too long. Besides, the Vikings were careful housekeepers and material goods were scarce. When they abandoned the place they would have carried off everything of value. The acid soil of the area took care of the rest, destroying even bones.

Only two identifiable objects were found: an iron nail of the Viking type and a small soapstone spindle whorl. This second find was particularly important because it indicated that the Vikings had brought women with them. Spinning was strictly women's work.

At about the same time that Dr. Ingstad was digging in Newfoundland, a very different type of evidence for Leif's voyage was being examined at the Yale University Library. The library had received a map, apparently drawn in 1440, fifty-two years before Columbus' voyage. In the upper left-hand corner of the map was a remarkably accurate representation of Greenland, but even more significant was a three-lobed island to the west of Greenland. This land mass was labeled Helluland, Markland, and Vinland, and an inscription stated that this was the land discovered by Bjarne and Leif. If the 1440 date proved to be correct, then the Vinland map, as it came to be called, contained the first known representation of North America, and provided strong confirmation for the claim that Leif Ericsson had discovered America.

The Vinland map was bound in with a medieval manuscript called "Tartar Relation," the hitherto unknown account of the travels of a Franciscan monk in China. The quality of the parchment, the watermarks, and the handwriting in the manuscript all indicated that the map and the "Tartar Relation" were prepared by the same hand at the same time. Yet the two did not seem to fit together properly. After years of uncertainty the Yale Library obtained a copy of a standard medieval historical reference book called *Mirror of His-*

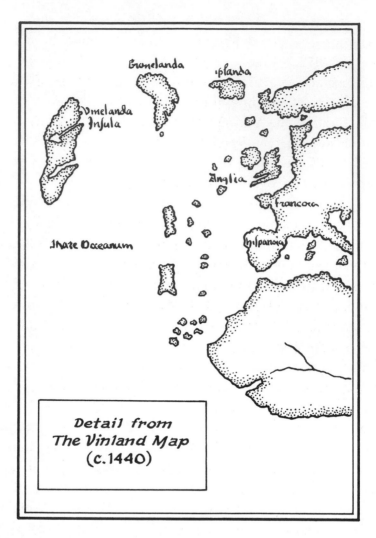

Detail from
The Vinland Map
(c.1440)

tory. It was obvious to the experts in ancient documents that the map, "Tartar Relation," and the historical work had, at one time, all been bound together in a single volume, not an unusual practice in medieval times.

The experts now felt that they could reconstruct the history of the Vinland map. It was drawn about 1440 by an unknown monk in Basel, Switzerland. The parchment came from that time and that area. At about the same time a long Church council was being held

146

at Basel. It was the sort of event which would have attracted church-
men from Scandinavia. One of them carried an old map, dating back
to the time when the memory of the voyages of Leif Ericsson was
still fresh. The unknown scribe looked at this map and included the
Vinland and Greenland information on the world map he was preparing for the use of the Basel scholars.

The representation of Vinland in a 1440 map was astounding
to modern scholars, but it is doubtful if the monk who copied the
map considered it important. On the map Vinland is shown only as a
large island in the Atlantic. There is no indication that anyone knew
it was part of a continent. Why should this scribe be excited about
another Atlantic island? There were plenty of them; the Vinland
map shows several. The difference, of course, was that the other
islands were legendary; Vinland was not.

Numerous objections have been raised to the authenticity of
the Vinland map, but the vast majority of scholars hold that the map
was drawn a half century before Columbus' voyage. Apparently
Columbus had never seen the map or anything like it, or even heard
rumors of Vinland. He collected all sorts of tales about lands to the
west before he set out, and even made a trip to Iceland, but in the
records of his research the name Vinland is not mentioned. Besides,
he would not have been interested in northern islands; Columbus
was trying to sail clear around the world to Asia.

No one should really be surprised that the Vikings discovered
America. Indeed, it would have been more surprising if they had
not.

To the medieval European the Vikings were barbaric raiders.
In medieval prayers the Viking is one of the list of natural disasters
Christians asked God to protect them from. It is true that the Norse
were robbers and killers, but really no more brutal in the treatment
of their enemies than the nobles of Europe, for it was a bloody time.
The Vikings were just more successful so their savagery was widespread and well-known.

But the Vikings were much more than bloodthirsty pirates. They were excellent traders and businessmen, resourceful colonizers and explorers, and the greatest sailors the world has ever known. From earliest times the Norse had lived close to the sea, but they did not discover the sailing ship until around A.D. 600. Prior to that, their ships had been powered by the strong backs and arms of rowers. Such oar-driven ships were unsuited to long voyages, so the Vikings remained close to their Scandinavian homeland.

About the time the Vikings were perfecting their sailing techniques, something else happened that allowed them to roam more freely—the weather became warmer. It is now believed that the earth's climate undergoes long-term cyclic changes. Why this happens is unknown, but historical records and the investigations of specialists in the study of ancient climates indicate that around the year 800 northern areas warmed significantly. Harbors were ice-free for longer periods and dangerous icebergs were absent from sea lanes.

In 874 the Norse began moving to Iceland and by the year 930 the population of the island may have been nearly 20,000. In 900 a Viking driven off course discovered land to the northwest of Iceland and named it the Gunnbjorn Islands, after himself. Nothing more was heard of this land until 982 when one of the most hot-tempered residents of northwest Iceland got himself banished for three years after killing one of his neighbor's sons in a dispute.

This man was Eric the Red. He made use of his time in exile to explore the land of the northwest. Eric found an enormous but uninviting island. As he sailed southward he came to habitable areas. There Eric and his men passed the period of exile in hunting and exploring. Life was hard, but there was plenty of game available and good grass for pasture. Most importantly, it offered the independent Vikings more freedom than they could find in already crowded Iceland. When the time of his banishment ended Eric went back to Iceland, determined to return to this great island and start a colony.

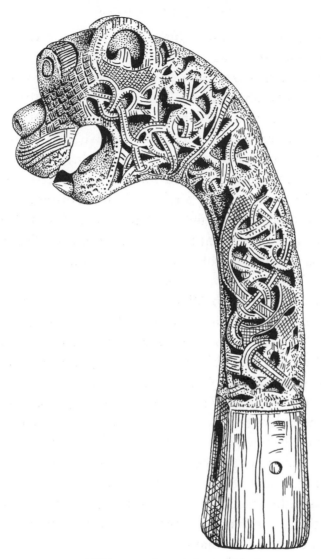

Viking carving of dragon head

He named the land Greenland, although even in that warmer era it was not particularly green, but, in the words of the sagas, "he felt that many would go there if it had a good name."

How right he was. In 986, twenty-five ships with 500 to 700 settlers aboard sailed for Eric's Greenland. One of the colonists was a man named Herjulf who was unaware that his son Bjarne would soon come looking for him.

When Bjarne finally found his father, after an extensive detour, and told his tales of land, and good rich land, even farther west, the story attracted great interest, particularly among the restless sons of Eric the Red who must have been eager to live up to their father's accomplishments and establish reputations of their own.

Leif knew that once he sailed away from the coast of Greenland he would have to go only a relatively short distance across the open sea before he caught sight of land again. From then on he could sail down the coast until he reached Vinland. There was no doubt that his ship could make the voyage; it was the same ship in which Bjarne had already made the trip.

Aside from landing in Vinland there is one other important incident in Leif Ericsson's life that is worth mentioning. According to some of the tales it was Leif who introduced Christianity to Greenland. Leif was probably born in Iceland and raised in Greenland, but, the sagas say, in 999 he visited Norway and was converted to Christianity by King Olaf I. Slowly the Vikings, once the scourge of Christendom, were being converted. But the fierce old gods were still worshipped in the outer fringes of the Viking world. The king gave Leif the mission of carrying the new faith to distant Greenland —no easy task since it was stoutly resisted by his hot-tempered and old-fashioned father who, after all, was leader of the Greenland colony. But the young man succeeded, and in short order the Greenland Vikings became Christians.

Leif's passage to Vinland was, it seems, a remarkably easy one. He stepped ashore in a country where the grass was rich and the rivers were filled to overflowing with fish. And then there was the legendary wine. The sagas contain this story: One of the members of Leif's crew, a German named Tyrk, wandered off by himself. When the others found him, Tyrk was flat on the ground babbling in his native tongue, an unintelligible language to the Vikings. Tyrk was quite drunk. When he sobered up enough to recall the Norse language he told the others that he had found grapes. Because Tyrk had grown up in the wine-producing areas of Germany he knew very well what to do with his find.

Again we are confronted with the problem of wine. The only Viking settlement has been found in Newfoundland, but grapes do not grow there and never have. What was Tyrk drinking? Dr. Ingstad believes that the German had found berries, not grapes. Berry juice left to ferment will produce quite an intoxicating beverage. This theory is strengthened by mention that Leif's men chopped down "grape trees" and brought them to Greenland where wood was a valued commodity. Grapes do not grow on trees; berries do.

Through the centuries Leif Ericsson has gained the nickname "Leif the Lucky" and apparently he was lucky in everything he did. His brother Thorvald was not. When, during his expedition to Vinland, Thorvald was struck down by an arrow, his last words were supposed to have been: "We have won a fine and fruitful country, but will hardly be allowed to enjoy it."

For a time Thorvald's final judgment seemed too pessimistic. Sixteen years after his death a large expedition under Thorfinn Karlsfini sailed to Vinland and established a colony. But, in the end, Thorvald's gloomy prediction proved correct, for the Viking effort to establish a permanent colony failed.

Some intriguing questions remain. How extensive was the Viking colonization? How long did it last? And why did it end? The Vinland map sheds a certain amount of light on the first two questions. Norse records mention cryptically that Bishop Eric Gnupsson set out for Vinland. The map contains additional information on this visit. It says, the "legate of the Apostolic See and Bishop of Greenland and the neighboring regions arrived in this truly vast and very rich land" and that he "remained a long time in both summer and winter." Scholars have placed the bishop's visit in the year 1117, over a hundred years after Leif landed in Vinland. So the colonies

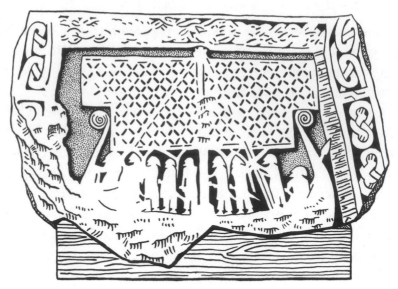

Viking relief of ship

lasted at least that long, and to command an extended visit by so important a church official they must have been fairly large.

Two factors probably brought an end to the Norse adventure in Vinland; repeated attacks by the natives and a gradually worsening climate. The sagas call the natives Skraelings, and they are described as "swarthy men, and ill-looking, and the hair of their heads was ugly. They had great eyes, and were broad of cheek." This is what Indians or, more likely, Eskimos might have looked like to the Norse. Shortly after the Vikings came to Vinland there were massive migrations of Eskimos to Greenland. The same sort of mass movements may have taken place in North America. The Skraelings were hostile, and although they were less advanced than the Vikings, their attacks constituted a real threat to the continued existence of the isolated colonies.

The climate, which had warmed around 800, began to cool again. Later tales from Greenland mention icebergs in the sea lanes, an unknown danger in earlier times. The growing season in Greenland shortened and the Greenlanders became more and more dependent upon supplies from the European mainland. All the while, ice was making communication more difficult. From the middle of the fifteenth century on, no more is heard from Greenland.

It was not until the eighteenth century that Greenland was rediscovered. At first there was some hope of finding survivors, but there were none. Excavating graves at one of the Viking settlements, the explorers were able to determine the melancholy fate of the Greenlanders. The bodies in the graves had been frozen and thus were grotesquely well preserved. They showed the last of the Greenlanders had been a deformed and disease-riddled people—all the result of extreme malnutrition.

The Vikings of Vinland may also have died off when cold and ice cut their contact with the mother country, but no Viking burial grounds have yet been found in America. Or they may have returned before the darkness closed in, although there is no record of this. The fate of the Vinlanders is a fruitful area for future research.

Leif himself did not stay in the land he discovered. He returned to Greenland and spent the remainder of his life on the family farm at Brattahlid. Not long ago Eskimos now living at Brattahlid uncovered the remains of an ancient Viking church while digging the foundation for a new school. Archaeologists from the Danish National Museum who excavated the site of the church identified it as Thjodhild's Church, named after Leif's mother, at whose insistance it was built. The church is surrounded by a graveyard, but all the graves are unmarked.

It was customary to bury important members of the Viking community near the church wall. Knud Krogh, the archaeologist in charge of the excavations, speculates that five or six members of Leif's family may be there. Eric the Red could be one, although this is in doubt, since his dislike of the new faith is well known. Thjodhild is certainly there; it is her church. Leif and his son Thorkel, who inherited Brattahlid in turn, are also probably buried near the wall. Perhaps even the body of Leif's brother Thorvald, who had been

153

killed by Indians in Vinland, was ultimately returned to Brattahlid. There is recorded evidence that one of Leif's other brothers made an unsuccessful attempt to recover the body, and archaeologist Krogh believes that other Greenlanders voyaging to Vinland would have accomplished this task, for Greenlanders would go to great lengths to return bodies for proper burial. It seems that desolate Greenland is the final resting place of the discoverer of America and his far-roaming family.

INDEX

Index

THE AUTHOR

DANIEL COHEN claims that his interest in archaeology began at the age of five when he was scared half to death by a mummy on display at the Oriental Institute in Chicago. "Over the years my terror changed to curiosity, and curiosity to the realization that 'the thing' beneath those wrappings had once been a human being, like myself. What sort of a person had he been? What kind of life did he lead?" In SECRETS FROM ANCIENT GRAVES, Mr. Cohen answers such questions about peoples of the ancient world. He holds a journalism degree from the University of Illinois and has been a science writer all his professional life. He is currently managing editor of *Science Digest* magazine and has written articles for many magazines, as well as a previous book, MYTHS OF THE SPACE AGE. A native of Chicago, he and his wife now live in New York City.

THE ILLUSTRATOR

ELIZA MCFADDEN studied painting and drawing at the Cranbrook Academy Art School and majored in painting at the School of the Museum of Fine Arts in Boston. She also holds a B.S. degree in physics from the College of William and Mary. She has taught art classes for both children and adults, and her art work has been displayed in individual and group shows throughout New England. As an illustrator for the Department of Anthropology at the Peabody Museum, Harvard, she recently completed illustrations for a two-volume book on American archaeology. Born in Ann Arbor, Michigan, Miss McFadden lives in Cambridge, Massachusetts.